SON OF THE CHURCH

SON OF
THE CHURCH

BY

Louis Lochet

TRANSLATED BY

Albert J. LaMothe, Jr.

FIDES PUBLISHERS ASSOCIATION

CHICAGO 19, ILLINOIS

Library of Congress Catalog Card Number: 56-11631

Nihil Obstat: Rev. Roland G. Simonitsch, C.S.C., Ph.D.,
University of Notre Dame

Imprimatur: Leo A. Pursley, D.D.,
Apostolic Administrator of
the Diocese of Fort Wayne
in Indiana

 55

Manufactured by American Book–Stratford Press, Inc.

DEDICATION

The Virgin Mary
Queen of Apostles

St. Therese of the Child Jesus
Patroness of the Missions

CONTENTS

FOREWORD

THIS BOOK does not pretend to make a scientific contri-
bution to the consideration of the Church. It does not
seek to further theological research now in progress. It is
not the fruit of meditation on ideas or of reflection on
texts. It is born of life. Let us not expect of it an ordered
and complete exposition of the structure and the life of
the Church, for many essential things would be missing.

We have simply wished to bring out the testimony of
a man who works in the Church and who seeks to understand what he is doing by discovering what she is. Our
life has sought light. We needed this light so as not to
fall into lassitude or discouragement, into revolt or despair. We have not determined beforehand where all
this would lead us. And each time the light has shone
upon our life, it has brought us back to the mystery of
the Church. Of that we have retained what would permit us to shed light upon our actions, to sustain our
efforts and to direct our steps.

We are not recording the testimony of an exceptional

experience. These considerations are grafted onto everyday life and common experiences. Perhaps it is precisely because of this that they have been of service to others. Whether cry of suffering or song of joy, they find an echo in the hearts of those who work and struggle in the service of Christ in His brethren.

The more we went on, in fact, the more apparent it became to us that apostolic action, to keep its balance, without ending in exhaustion or becoming lost in incoherence, needs all the reflection of theologians, the whole light of Revelation, the entire movement of grace, the labor of all others, the prayer of all the saints, and, finally, the life of the whole Church. He who gives himself to it enters into the designs of God and, in the end, can no longer understand himself except in the action of God on His Church. This light has guided our research. It has spread slowly in three complementary directions.

At the very beginning, it is apostolic action itself which encourages reflection. It involves so many questions! And first of all, there is the enormous disproportion between the love of men which bears us up, between the immense desire to save humanity and to bring it together in unity, and the innate weakness of our actions which reach so few people and for so short a time. What are we doing that is worth the struggle? How is the drive which gives rise to our actions going to end? Man cannot disavow this love of what is human without disowning himself, and he cannot carry it through without going beyond himself. The love that wants to save can only come to a head by meeting up with the unique Savior, in Whom the impotent love of man for man is absorbed in the all-powerful love of God for man. We can do nothing that has a bearing on the goal we are pursuing

—which is catholic salvation—except in Jesus Christ, Savior of the world.

Yet, if it is God Who saves, what is required of us? What is the place of human activity in His plan of salvation? What is the importance and the efficacy of our mission to men? What is the meaning, the value of our apostolate? Here is the mystery of human activity which surpasses itself on entering the service of God, in order to enter into the universal and to participate in the eternal designs. To understand ourselves and to comprehend our activity, it is ultimately necessary to see ourselves in the sacred history in which His redemptive action is expressed: in His Church. Our activity finds its meaning and its value only in the Church, and for the Church, to the glory of Christ the Savior. Lacking that, it founders in absurdity and despair.

This goes for our whole selves. This activity in the Church, this insertion into her mystery is exacting. It calls forth and effects a *purification*. This involvement with the Church concerns not only our actions; it concerns our being: we are entirely part of her. Our life, our activity, our vocation all develop within the Church; we are living members of her. It is the very demands of the life of the Church that will bring with them the increase of the spiritual life. Thus, we can speak of spiritual purification not only beginning with the individual march of a soul to God, but also and especially, by reason of the collective requirements of the people of God. Our activity and our very soul are caught up in its history, and companions in this long march cross the desert, and in the multiple trials which mark the progress of God's people toward the Promised Land.

It is the Church, the Church of today, that demands

of us this purity of faith and generosity in giving. She has her own proper and actual requirements which we have to understand and accept. Our life grows in faith and our soul is purified by grace according to the twofold rhythm of our personal life and the collective life of the Church which gives the command. Grace is given us in her. We are made for her. We are fashioned by her. We are her children.

Thus, our spiritual effort appears as a *purification* of our activity and of our giving in the communal activity and offering of the Church to the Father. We make progress in life by means of a more intimate union with the Mystical Body of Christ, which is His Church. We are saints in the very measure in which we are His in her. But this adherence to the Church demands also purity in the way we look at her. If we are more completely united to the Church, it is because more and more we are discovering Jesus in her. Our purified look must no longer let itself stop at the veil of appearances but instead discover in the Church the design of God. What the Church bears in her that is provisional and incomplete nevertheless permits the faithful soul to catch a glimpse of and to guess at the adorable plan of definitive union of Bridegroom and Bride.

Purified in the Church and through her, the soul *contemplates* its Lord present in itself. Not only does the Church give it the Eucharist, in which it always finds Him present; but each of her Sacraments, each of her actions, everything by which we live and which we draw forth from her, bears for the soul a discreet and delightful reference to this union, already achieved inwardly, whose secret will be revealed to the world at the time of the Last Coming. Our activity in the Church is rich in contemplation if we know how to light it with faith and live it in expectation.

Activity in the Church, purification in the Church, contemplation in the Church, those are the three themes that recur incessantly in our reflections, because they make up our life. Engaging in activity in the Church demands the purification of our energies for her and in her; the purity of our views leads to contemplation. Realizing in this way that we owe her all that we are, we cannot do other than to turn to her as sons, for she is truly our Mother—she who has received everything from God to give it all to us—she in whom the Father communicates to us His life, through His Son, in the Spirit.

L. L.

1

TEMPTATIONS

OUR THINKING about the Church often begins with the difficulties we experience regarding her. A large part of our life may have been spent in a sort of peaceful possession of the Christian life in the Church. It is when we seek to communicate our faith and to spread Christian life that we encounter these difficulties. By a sort of transference, we view things at such times from the point of view of the unbeliever. Suddenly we see our faith as from the outside. What seems indisputable to us, because we were used to it, appears startling and sometimes scandalous to us. Ceremonies and chants which we liked without ulterior motive shock us because now we feel that they speak a strange language to those to whom we address ourselves. The attitudes of the Church, the ways of acting of Church people, we resent with the sensitivity of those on the outside. The more ardently we desire to draw them to Christ, living in the Church, the more we suffer as a result of everything in her that could lead away from Him; so that, by a strange paradox, it is sometimes those who devote themselves most generously to the service of the Church who become her severest critics.

This critical awareness of Church realities can result in improving our adherence, which becomes more reflective, and our action, which becomes more demanding, just as it may also result in vain recriminations or dangerous ruptures. At all events, it is a trial, a crisis in our belonging to the Church. We are entirely taken up in it.

1. *The critical age.*

It is a little like family life. When the adolescent discovers his own personality and becomes involved in the world of work, he sees his own family in a new light. For the first time he sees it as from the outside. He measures and judges it. His first position when faced with the family environment risks being a severe one—a reaction against what he has received, a criticism of things whose limitations he discovers; this is a crisis of the family spirit.

This crisis can result in a rupture if a man chooses himself in rejecting what he has received from his people. But it can also develop into progress, if the setback he receives with regard to his environment teaches him to appreciate its values, and if the man consents, by choice, to the living bonds in which the child grew up. It is this clear consent to his origins that is the real surpassing of the crisis of adolescence in adult years.

Thus it is with us, with respect to the Church. The modern Christian acquires an awareness of the Church which permits him to question her. The moment we enter upon apostolic activity becomes a critical moment. Here it is no longer the family spirit that is on trial, it is the spirit of faith. For it is not a question of finding reason for the Church, but rather of recognizing ourselves in her and of entering more deeply into her mystery so as to become more totally involved in it. It is not a question of being her judges, but rather of accepting in all lucidity to be her children. One may say that there is no adult in the apostolate who has not surmounted this crisis. But what I resent at this moment, others resent along with me. This crisis that I am undergoing, we are undergoing together. It is not just a personal crisis—it is a collective crisis. It is a critical age in the life of the Church.

2. *The awakening of the world.*

Like all the great realities of the Church, this crisis bears a hidden relationship to the general life of the world. It is a general crisis of this world that we have called the modern world, which comes to a head in the Church and which must without doubt, become untangled in her. What is taking place at the present time is not only a becoming aware on the part of Christians of the realities of the Church; it is a similar reflection by the world and the Church on their own principles which leads them to a stiffer because more thought-out, opposition to one another. Age of thought and of criticism in order to become the age of building and of technology—such is the characteristic of the modern world.

Everything that has been lived, thought and built by preceding ages, without ulterior motive and as it were naïvely, has become subject to re-thinking and criticism. Thought has become reflection and people have criticized reason. The intellect has become lost in the search for itself. Science has become reflective, and the methods of the sciences have been developed. We have a whole world of new sciences born, which have scientific methods of research. Political institutions, economic realities, social life, have been considered in themselves, analyzed, and taken apart mentally, before being so in reality.

Men have made and are making revolutions; and not only revolutions of forces and of men, but revolutions of ideas. Men have circled the globe and almost circled the universe. Man has pushed back by a thousand centuries the history of mankind. Man discovers himself in space and in time. Humanity, in two centuries, has entered into an extraordinary phase of the development of its knowledge. For the first time, man speaks of mankind, of the earth and of the world. He judges himself and takes his measurements in the universe. He has become brilliant.

The brilliant man, the man fortified by science and by techniques, has turned toward the earth in order to conquer it. Everywhere he has set to work to make the earth a more human place. Great works have been undertaken. From one end of the world to the other there is communication—everything has become world-wide. Economics is world-wide, politics and wars themselves are world-wide. The advances of science and art emerge in everyone's consciousness. Mankind feels a painful need for unity; its members develop and grow, their bonds multiply and expand, its face changes, its awareness is enriched, its projects are immense. Man is experiencing a crisis of growth.

3. *Awakening of the Church.*

The Church too is in full growth—growth in thought and growth in action. Father H. Clerissac used to deplore the reflective attitude of modern spirituality. It can be regretted, but it cannot be avoided. Modern man is reflective even in his spiritual life. He no longer knows how to live in grace except by examining himself on the manner in which it acts and in which he reacts to it. Prayer itself has become an exercise; it has been subjected to methods. People are in the process of organizing the apostolate. They are discovering that it rests on a scientific knowledge of environments and on precise techniques. Theological and scriptural research has accepted scientific methods.

There is no domain of the Church's life, of her prayer, of her thought and of her activity, that has not undergone within a century, through the efforts of reflection, a profound renovation. Her zone of influence has indisputably increased. An apostolic current, from the Middle Ages to our day, passes through the Church with astonishing power and persistence. The search for perfection, which had initially been oriented to retreat from the world, in the hermitical or monastic life, now urges the most generous souls into the midst of the world.

Through the mendicant orders of the 13th century, through the apostolic orders of the 16th and 17th centuries, up to the latest orientations of modern spirituality, there flows a powerful current which turns the forces of sanctity toward the evangelization of the world. In the wake of the explorers and sometimes before them, missionaries have covered the entire surface of the earth.

More and more men are thinking and living in a catholic manner. An immense love of man, of all men, comes to light, manifests itself, bursts forth through the work of the Church which has covered the world and which pursues every human misery on a universal scale. The Gospel has been translated into all languages and almost all dialects, from Africa to the Far East. Churches are being built, a native clergy is developing in practically all corners of the globe, with a rapidity unknown in past centuries.

And still we are not satisfied. We are less satisfied than ever. A new passion, it seems, a new orientation, and as it were a new dimension of our apostolic sense have come to light in us: a sense of the masses, a concern for the masses, a love for the masses. It is not enough to create here and there, even geographically everywhere, churches and Hierarchies. It is not enough to help here and there, even everywhere, a few of the most miserable among men. It is all men that we love, it is all men that must be saved. Yes, it is this charity of God which wants to save all men, *"qui vult omnes homines salvos fieri,"* [1] it is this which flows in us and gives us no rest until we have reached them all.

The Church is not reserved for an international elite, the Church is made for all men of all nations. This sense of mass is like a third dimension of the apostolic sense, like a depth in humanity, like a new advance into the bosom of the world to be saved . . . and we can see no end to it. But now the masses of all countries, of the Far East, and of Africa, and of Europe, the largest part of the human group, are workers, are the world of labor.

---

[1] *Tim.* 2:4.

This world which was born in the last century unto an awareness of itself, and which has discovered by a sort of mysterious presentiment its international unity, acts in the world with an immense drive whose pressure rocks the march of events.

4. *More conscious opposition between the world and the Church.*

The drama of our time, the great drama that grips us, is that at the very moment when the Church becomes more vividly aware of her catholic unity, at the very moment when her apostolic sense makes her feel more keenly perhaps than ever before the need for carrying the Gospel to the masses, to the world of workers, to the modern world formed by labor, at this very moment, the world finds itself formed outside the Church, closed to her influence, and as if that were not enough, in large part arrayed against her.

The conflict between the spirit of the world and the Church has always existed, but never have so clear a reflection, so definitive an awareness on both sides of positions and opposition, made it so acute. Between this formidably active and numerous world that builds and runs machines, that works in factories, that furrows the world and exploits it, between this world of work and technical progress, and the Church as expressed in worship and parish life, we sadly perceive a profound misunderstanding—more than a misunderstanding, a secret tension—worse alas, a terrible opposition.

There is misunderstanding, because the workers take us for what we are not. In reality, they do not know us. They no longer know who we are. They scarcely know that we exist. Perhaps it is our fault . . . we are not close to hand. The veritable antiquity of the rites, the customs and the costumes, does not permit them to guess that the Church is ever young and bears a message of love that is strangely new and necessary even today. How are they to go about looking for the indispensable secret of the human community of tomorrow in one who seems to them to belong in so many ways, to a dated past?

Semitic in her ancestors, Roman in her origins, medieval in her customs, the Church seems very far from the workaday world. How we suffer from that! Our ecclesiastical attitudes do not allow the eternal timeliness of the Gospel to show up enough. The world of work can no longer recognize in us the Christ Who loves it, Who speaks to it, Who calls it. And yet it needs this more than ever! We would like to let the masks fall. Let us recognize one another! May this world which for so long has sought gropingly for justice for the poor, deliverance of captives, the universal love of all that is human, for peace, find all these blessings to which it aspires, in Jesus hidden in the Church.

Who then will know how to say the words and do the things that will remove this tragic misunderstanding, this residue of so many lies which weighs upon the world?

But there is more than that. In reality, there is much more than a misunderstanding. It would be puerile to believe that a change of garb or a change of language would suddenly make this entire mass recognize the Church as a mother too long forgotten. It is not simply a case of translating the Gospel and of giving it a modern expression, for people to accept it. Between the modern world with its own dynamism, and the very life of the Church in her essential message, there is a secret tension, a profound divergence, a sort of latent incompatibility. They face in opposite directions. Even when they consider the same thing, they do not look at it in the same way, and ultimately, they do not see it as the same thing. How could they understand one another? Not only do they not speak the same language, they do not even have the same ideas.

The world of labor and technology thinks to organize the world, to transform it and exploit it, for the temporal happiness of man. It looks upon things not so much to know and admire them but to make use of them. It looks upon men in order to organize their relationships in such a way that each has what he needs. It studies their physical organism in order to take care of them and preserve their health. It studies their psychology to keep them balanced and happy. It makes use of everything to make them happy on earth. It does not always succeed in doing so; it does not often succeed in doing so. Who could reproach it for persistently straining to do so?

The Church announces an eternal salvation. She knows that all that is in time runs out and passes along with it. She invites people to detach themselves from what will some day have to be left behind. She looks upon the things of this world as a reflection of eternity, insofar as they announce and prepare for Heaven. She does not install herself on earth; she passes through it to go toward her Kingdom, which is in Heaven. She looks upon men as voyagers toward the City of God.

She does not refuse the organization of earthly life, the struggle for happiness here below, the care of health, the desire for justice and peace on earth. She even works for those things. She asks that men work for them. But she unceasingly invites men to go beyond all that, so as to tend toward the eternal goods which in the light of faith, are the only true goods, the only ones that last, the only ones that satisfy the heart of man. She brings the world a message of happiness, but an eternal happiness which teaches one to go beyond all the goods of earth and to detach one's heart from them. "Blessed are the poor in spirit, for theirs is the Kingdom of Heaven."

The world accuses her of turning men aside from the urgent tasks of earthly organization, of disgusting them, discouraging them, of detaching them from the common labor which is to assure happiness to all. Christians no longer believe that, because they know too well that the world will always be unhappy and that even its happiness is not worth a great deal. Perhaps they do not even wish it, and one may ask if they are not counting a little on earthly misery to make people desire the goods of Heaven, if they are not keeping this wound open to make people want the doctor. The world secretly feels that the Church does not enter wholly into its project for happiness. She does not understand it, and eventually opposes it. The world accuses the Church of preventing men from working at their happiness; they not only treat her as a stranger, they treat her as a nuisance and often as an enemy.

The Church accuses the world of turning men aside from the only real happiness. According to this view, the world captures human energies, the lights of intellect and the physical forces, the whole impetus of the heart, for an ever-greater production of earthly goods which are consumed and used up, which are incapable of fulfilling desire, which only arouse greed, incite jealousies, hatreds and conflicts, and deceive the hunger of mankind made for the infinite. The Church accuses the world of leading men astray, of deceiving them, of depriving them of real happiness.

And so, this more lively awareness that mankind has obtained in the modern world, of its capacities for knowledge, of its possibilities of production, and this internal development of the Church which has made her discover in a more well-defined way her structure, her dimensions and her life, have resulted in a more conscious, more lively and more cruel opposition. At the very moment when the Catholic Church feels deepening in her heart the desire to carry Christ to the masses of workers spread throughout the entire world, these masses become aware of themselves outside the Church and against her. They were born far from the Church, in the shops; they have grown up in misery, and now that they are becoming aware of their strength, they assert themselves in refusal. Those who lacked God terribly, now deny God. Not only have they not found Him, but they reject Him. Privation has become negation. The search for temporal goods has become a negation of the eternal. This God Whom they do not know they fight as an enemy of the people. The movement of thought and action which carries along the totality of the working world and in which it becomes aware of itself, is an explicitly atheistic, a militantly atheistic, movement. It rejects God and would like the very thought of Him, and His name, to disappear from the world, for they seem to it to be the greatest obstacle to the happiness of man.

The drama, for every apostle, is to enter into a world so cruelly divided. Those with whom we rub elbows are the furthest away from us. Someday we must finally realize that the very ones we want most to reach and touch are the most opposed to us; those to whom we most desire to speak no longer understand our language and do not want to hear us.

5. *Temptation to discouragement.*

The first of our temptations in the face of this inability of the Church to make herself understood by the modern world is certainly a temptation to discouragement. How to announce the Gospel? The language we speak, and not only the words, but the rites, gestures, attitudes, mentality, are for this world a foreign tongue. Everything that used to speak to the spirit, to the imagination and to the heart, has become an undecipherable message. "I am aware of this fact," writes Cardinal Suhard: "the totality of our people no longer thinks in a Christian way; there is between them and the Christian community an abyss which means that, to reach them, we must leave our homes and go to theirs." [2] Leaving our homes means not only changing houses and neighborhoods, it means quitting a whole world of habits and attitudes, exterior and interior, social and personal, to be born again in a new world, share its conditions, its aspirations, its life—to be *of* it. Otherwise, we run up against a blank wall.

Perhaps we work for the Church but alongside this new world. We sense, we see, we know that beyond those who are still capable of entering into the social life of the Church, into her morals and her rites, a new world, which is the working world, remains without Christ, because we have not reached its heart. Because of not see-

---

[2] *Carnets du Cardinal Suhard*, Paris, Bonne Presse, p. 30.

ing, knowing, imagining, what has to be done to reach it, more than one person, cleric or lay, one day experiences the feeling of his impotence and the temptation to a kind of disillusionment regarding the possibilities of the Church in the face of the modern world.

This temptation can result in a rupture. If we despair of doing something with the Church, we risk trying to do something outside her. It may also end up in a sort of slightly passive resignation which is a secret form of despair; we work in the Church without really believing in the success of the Church. We no longer believe in the salvation of the world. Faith in salvation seems an illusion of youth. It is no longer union with the Church that is threatened, but love for the Church, joy in belonging and confidence in her leaders. How are we to save? Because of the lack of a clear vision of what has to be done, how many lives fall back! What unemployed energies, how many people discouraged before beginning, how many possibilities not utilized, how many opportunities missed! Who can say what generosity and heroism on the part of youth faith in the salvation of the world, in the salvation of mankind, could give rise to?

To render Faith in the Church, to give this certitude that her work is in the process of saving the world, this world that we love, to show in faith how she is working, operating, laboring, progressing, in order to save mankind; how this is being done at the price of all our efforts and all our lives given to Christ—nothing is more urgent. It is this appeal we must cause to be heard in order to raise up courage, to bring about belonging and giving in joy and in hope.

6. *Temptation of evasion.*

It is our faith in the power of the Church, in the vitality of the Church, in the necessity of the Church for the modern world, in her capacity for reaching and transforming it, which awakens in us the apostolic sense. It is because we have believed that we have begun to speak. But it is not a matter only of words; we must announce the Gospel by our whole lives. No word is suitable except by the Incarnation of the Word. We must enter into this world, however far off it may be, we must live in it, and not only by a sort of local displacement, changing neighborhoods and dwelling-places, but by a psychological expatriation, changing mentality and customs. That is the most difficult part.

To reach those we are seeking we have to be one of them, members of the community and the neighborhood, in a solidarity of destiny with the aspirations of the world in the making: all in all to give them all to Jesus Christ. We must, finally, enter—not by a fiction, verbally, not by means of discourses and protestations of sympathy, but with heart and in actions, at the price of our whole lives, in the aspirations of the world that is working for justice and peace.

Meanwhile, in this effort, which is the essential part of the missionary effort, a new temptation lies in ambush for us: it is to enter so totally into the world that we are absorbed in it, to espouse its aspirations so perfectly that we are limited by them, to live by its reactions so perfectly that we prevent ourselves from going beyond them. It is to be not only in the world, but of the world. It is, to sum up, to seek only, or at least principally, the goods of this world; it means that the center of interest, the desire of the heart, the impetus of action, the sense of life, are placed at the level of initiating a better temporal order, rather than that of announcing the Kingdom of Heaven. Therefore, the apostle of Christ, has become a militant for social justice, for the promotion of the worker's cause, or for international peace. Because these goods are the highest one may desire on earth, because they require the total gift of oneself, because they place the objective of a better world before activity, they are able to furnish a sort of earthly decalcomania of the Kingdom of Heaven.

It remains that, if the apostle goes after nothing more than that, if he enters totally into the world's drive toward the building of a better world, he no longer carries in him that necessity for going beyond what is the essential part of the evangelic message. Perhaps he brings with him a project of salvation, but it is the salvation of man by man, and not that of the sinful world by Christ Jesus. He has lost the meaning of his message. He has abandoned that which is disconcerting and mysterious in the Gospel. He has lost his savor; he no longer announces Christ, he has vacated the Cross, he is merely announcing man and the elements of the world. He has lost the meaning of the Incarnation; for if he is a man among men, he is no longer bringing them the presence of God among them.

From that time forward, he can no longer get along with the Church. He is no longer able to hear her. They no longer understand each other. The very mission of the Church, her goal and her order of march are to announce the invisible blessings God has reserved for those whom He loves; it is to give divine life, to proclaim the salvation of man by God. The Church cannot enter whole-heartedly into the building up of a human order which would be sufficient for the happiness of men; she knows that this is a myth, a mirage that leads astray, an illusion that leads to despair. She preaches the only happiness that is able to satisfy the heart of man, and that surpasses everything earthly. For her to deny that would be to deny herself.

That is why she will never recognize as apostolate the activity of the militant which aims only at a human order and a justice without grace. Could it be the tragic lot of the militant of modern times not to be understood by the Church for whom he is working? Such rather is the decisive trial that puts him squarely up against a supernatural choice. It is here that he encounters the Cross. It is here that he must choose and know whether he wants to do a human work or accomplish the designs of God in the mystery of the Church. Only a viewpoint of faith and an act of hope can keep in the Church the one who wants to act on the world's destiny.

How then to find one's way, this narrow way that leads to life? Are these the only two possible attitudes to remain in the Church just as she is, not to pose problems and to take note with resignation, or with despair, of her separation from the great currents of life of the workaday world—or else to pass over to the world, to enter with enthusiasm into its constructive evolution and to become progressively more separated from the Church and her supernatural plans?

7. *Temptation to treason.*

We have to be in the world without being of the world. Such is the difficult assignment Christ has left to

His apostles. We must never relinquish either of these two terms whose union constitutes the mystery of the Incarnation: fully man, without any cheating, and fully of God, without failing. Immanent and transcendent, all the divine in the human. It is the very transcendence of the divine which permits immanence. It is because the life Christ came to bring is a divine life that it is able to penetrate without deforming them all mentalities and all human civilizations. But herein is where the last and the most subtle, the most actual and widespread of the temptations against the Church lies in ambush for us.

Yes, we must bring to this world in the making, the re-discovery of God. We have to make the exigencies of divine life and the appeals of divine love penetrate all human realities. But precisely in order to maintain the fully divine character of the message to be borne, must we not disaffiliate it from the Church, which in her long historical career, has been found to be as it were marked and impregnated with human mentality, outworn expressions, disputable institutions? To return to the purely divine, or if you will, to the pure Gospel—temptations of Evangelism.

Thus we see flourishing at the present time a swarm of different sects, which pre-empt to their profit the profound need for religious life of a humanity deprived of God. The very purity of their drive toward God claims to rest on their refusal of a Church contaminated by her connivance with the world. Those who have as yet done nothing are hardly the ones to hold out clean hands. They are pure because they have no history. This need for purity is a seductive argument, when it is a question of religious renewal. Here it is not a question of suppressing the Church, by renouncing the religious aspirations of man, but to do better than she in her own field, which is that of religion, to supplant her by going beyond her, to replace her while pretending to serve her, to seize by fraud that which belongs to her, in a word to betray her.

This temptation may also catch unawares Christians, militants, even priests: not to quit the Church in order to adhere to a new sect, which can happen, but to carry on in the bosom of the Church as if the evangelization of the world were to be accomplished by bringing it the Church's goods . . . but outside her structures. The dispute between the modern world and the Church must be settled at her expense. It is always her customs and her laws, her attitudes and her institutions even, which must yield before the demands of adaptation. The actions of the Church and her language, her Liturgy and her Sacraments, being for the most part no longer understood, people must come to the point of dreaming of a religion, a life of grace and prayer . . . which do without all that, a religion of the heart, spontaneous prayer, life with Christ without common liturgy, without sacramental demands. At least, since rites and language are in man's very nature, it will be necessary to rediscover everything, reinvent everything, starting with the needs of the concrete man of such and such a milieu and epoch. Obedience to the Hierarchy, submission to laws, seem impossible in such an attitude. And that which is valid in it risks hiding the extent to which it compromises the very essence of the Church.

It is evident, indeed. No longer to believe that the Catholic Church is capable of bearing the message of Christ and divine life to the ears and heart of the modern world, is no longer to believe in her. We must not hide that from ourselves: such is really the profound meaning of the difficulties we are encountering—it is a crisis of our faith in the Church.

It is relatively easy to unmask errors, more difficult to define truth. If we are neither to remain in the Church as she is, despairing at the wall which separates her from the workaday world, nor pass over to the world, leaving the Church behind, nor adopt a religious life outside the Church structures, what are we to do?

It is not without point to remark first of all that what constitutes the error of these positions is what is excessive in them. Their heresy is in being separated. Their appeal, that which renders them more or less tempting, is that they possess a portion of truth. It is therefore necessary to rejoin to the unity of Catholic truth that which is correct in each of these concrete positions. It is true that we must keep the structures of the Church; it is in them and through them that we are to penetrate the world. It is true that we must once more go forth with a missionary impetus to penetrate this new world. It is true, finally, that, while preserving the structures of the Church, we must watch to see that her life is adapted, as always in the course of the centuries, to the exigencies of an evangelization which once again demands a translation of the Gospel. For that we have to have faith in the Church, in her vitality, in her divine mission. The Church has a message that is necessary for the world. She is still capable of delivering it.

We must also have faith in man himself, creature of God, capable of God, open to the life of God, in all the periods of his history, in all the states of his civilization. We must enter with confidence into the life of the world and into the stream of history, being assured that to respond to their most profound requests is to guide them to the Church. We must have faith in the Church, with the assurance that her structures are large enough, her vitality rich enough to assimilate in Christ all the resources of the world and the riches of history. Whence "the necessity of a double consent in the Church: the fundamentally necessary consent of life to be placed within the structure, without which we would have run in vain and life would not be the life of the Church; that of the structure to accede to the demands and the increases of life, without which, without being firm on its foundation, we would not run at all and the Church, faithful to her fundamental constitution, would fail to fulfil her mission." [3]

8. *Temptation against faith in the mystery of the Church.*

Let us simply admit that this solution, in the drawing-board stage, is far from having resolved all the difficulties of those who are building, and that the indication of the road on a map does not always suffice for us to find this road again in the forest.

It is easy to think of this co-adaptation of the structures of the Church to the life of the modern world . . . but how much more difficult to carry it out. Knowing how to adapt and submit oneself each day, to submit oneself and to advance, is a mystery of obedience whose weight bears down on all those who labor. How many times, while thus holding firmly to all that is of the Church and her traditions, and holding out our hand to this whole world that escapes us and that we must

---

[3] Congar, *"Jalons pour une théologie du laicat,"* Paris, Ed. du Cerf, 1953, p. 310.

not let go of, have we felt the sorrowful division of the Cross. Such is the situation of the apostle. The temptation is to let go of one or the other of the extremes that have to be joined, to quit the Cross. Nevertheless, here more than anywhere else, the words of St. John apply: "He who does the truth comes to the light." It is in accepting this saddening situation, this tension between the world in which we live and the Church of whom we are, which are separated in history and united in our hearts, that we will be able to grasp, by living it, the mystery of the Church.

Despite everything, it would still be little, if we did not experience the feeling that even when we suffer for them, these men will perhaps be lost. The theologian experiences a sort of intellectual satisfaction, when he has figured out the direction in which the solution of the Church's problems is to be sought. As men, as apostles, we experience a constant anguish at realizing that the solutions found demand enormous delays before being carried out, that it takes generations to start to do what we see is necessary. Two or three generations of worker misery were needed for us to feel in our flesh and in our heart this tragic break with the world of labor. How many more are going to be required still for this awareness to pass into actions, for these plans to develop into construction.

When we begin to do something, will we not get there too late, with two generations of delay, faced with a new world that will have been fashioned without us? Each day that passes, lives end that shall not have known the light; there are men who die to whom we shall not have shown, in the Church, the true face of Christ; there are human generations that depart, near and yet so far away from us, without our having been able to deliver to them the message which saves through this thickness of oversights and errors that chokes out the sound of our voices. Must we resign ourselves to that? Must we accept having lost so much time? Are there in the plan of God, sacrificed generations?

9. *The progress of the Faith.*

These questions, which constrain us, force us to place ourselves finally on the true level, which is the universal level, the catholic level, of God's plan for the world. The best way to understand nothing, to live in doubt and end up in despair, is to see everything in the light of our own selves, to separate ourselves, to see ourselves apart, outside the whole, and to think that the destiny of the Church is reducible to our particular difficulty, and that our impotence is a sign of hers. The only way to understand ourselves, to understand our work and that of our generation, is to see ourselves in the big picture, to see our times in the eternity of time and our particular difficulties in the grand design of God. We must not minimize the difficulty. We must enlarge it to fit the proportions of the world, and bring our case into the mystery of the Church. "Instead of more or less confusing her with ourselves, let us on the contrary apply ourselves, without looking for personal triumph therefrom, to become blended with her." [4]

For, basically, it is to this that we have to come; the great scandal is not only the divorce between the Church and the modern world, it is simply the opposition of the Church and the world through all the centuries. The

---

[4] de Lubac, *Méditation sur l'Eglise*, Paris, Aubie, p. 217.

great scandal is not only the weakness and as it were the impotence of the Church in the face of the contemporary world, it is the weakness, the laughable littleness of the plan of God in the face of the history of the world, it is the disproportion of sacred history in the face of history proper, it is the mystery of the Incarnation continued in the Church. For it is of this that we must finally think—that there have been men on earth for millions of years and that sacred history, from Abraham to Pius XII, adds up to little more than four thousand years. It is that hundreds of billions of men have lived, have suffered and have died, are now living, suffering and dying, without having heard of Christ; and there is not one among them who leaves us indifferent, not one for whom we would not have shed our blood, not one, we believe, for whom God Himself was not willing to spill His Blood.

Such is our faith. This incident, minute in the eyes of history, this incident about which the historians of the time scarcely spoke on the margin of history, this swirl of a few Jews around a prophet called Jesus Whom they crucified, is the center of the world's history, and His death personally concerns all men. This sacred history, the history of the tiny Jewish people during two thousand years before Jesus, and the history of the Church for two thousand years after, affect the very history of the world and give to the world the key to its destiny.

The great temptation, the latent rationalization of all our difficulties and of all our discouragements, is to see only what we are doing and not what God is doing. What we do hides from us what God does. It is a lack of faith. It is a short, narrow, niggardly view of our activity and that of the Church, on the level of what we know of it in a human way and of what we can know of it through experience and history alone—a discouraging view. How tiny this Church is for the great plan she pursues! Is she capable even of embracing the mankind she wants to raise up in order to save it? Have we not erred in confiding our life to her, for the purpose of accomplishing our intimate desire for the salvation of the world?

There is only one issue, and that is faith—faith in the Church and faith in our vocation in the Church. The work of the Church is not just another undertaking that we might judge by human measurements; it is a plan of God; it is *the plan* of God for the world. We cannot understand nor grasp the meaning and catholic scope of our action, our life, our being, except by seeing them forever in the mystery of the Church.

2

THE MYSTERY OF THE CHURCH

No LONGER CAN we be content with an individual search for perfection. That is the grandeur and the torment of our age—an immense desire for the salvation of the world works in our hearts. We confide this desire to the Church. Is she capable of bringing it to fulfilment? Our enthusiasm in belonging, our generosity in action depend on the answer to this question.

To go to the heart of this problem, it is not enough to cast a more optimistic look on the results already achieved by the Church's action in the past, nor even to show how the promises of magnificent progress are evident in her. Always there will remain this actual and tragic disproportion between what she does and what should be done. It is not on the level of experience and history that we may hope to find a solution, but in the light of faith which brightens the meaning of the Church. To grasp it, we have to stand off a little not only to see the place of our activity in the Church, but to catch a glimpse of the Church's place in the plan of God.

1. *The Church, Mystical Body of Christ for the manifestation of God—Merciful Love.*

God has but one idea which commands the entire constitution of the world and all its history: to manifest Himself in His works. He creates for His glory. Through creation and through events, the features of the Divine Face progressively appear. The history of the world is an appearance of God in His works, a slow and solemn Epiphany.

In material creation across the depths of the heavens, with bold strokes, He makes a sketch of His power and of His immensity. But there is a more faithful image: man bears in himself the resemblance of the spirit which comprehends everything in unity; already there are some traits of the love which is ecstasy and gift of self. What is more, through grace are born in him the sources of a new life, the urging of a divine love; through a transfigured humanity, there breathes the most secret mystery—God is Love. This is the key to the organization of the world—it is a manifestation of love, a manifestation of God as Love.

But we have not said everything. God has something else to say about Himself that neither nature, nor man, nor even primal grace, have known how to express. Yet it is as it were, the most secret fiber of His very Love—His mercy. God is merciful love. He is not only the love which gives, but also the love that forgives. He is not only the Goodness which raises up, but that which raises up anew. He is not only the Creator Who leans over the abyss of nothingness to draw forth His creature, but the Father Who leans over the abyss of sin to raise up His child. All human history is arranged for the manifestation of the divine mercy; there will be a Redemption. Sin and its immense ravages is permitted it, in order to give the measure of the Divine Love, and as the ladder of Its mercy. The traits of Justice itself underscore the effusion of this merciful goodness.

The whole history of Israel is a progressive manifestation of this mercy of God toward His people. It is scanned by the refrain of Psalm 135: ". . . for his mercy endures forever." Humanity, represented by God's people, appears at each turn of its history as misery unceasingly renewed and unceasingly relieved, and God is He Who cannot resist the call of this distress even when it is born of sin, especially then, for it is more complete: "He considered their affliction when he heard their prayer." [1] His mercy extends from age to age and fills the earth. "The earth is full of the grace of the Lord." [2] The perennial nature of His mercy shows the very eternity of God. His proper characteristic is to be faithful. God is the Faithful One. The great idea of the Covenant is that of a free gift which is granted once and for all by God to humanity, and which remains unshakeable despite the wanderings and denials of the latter. Thus is demonstrated an eternal goodness, for it is absolutely above the fluctuations of time and the defections of the creature; it commits itself in that one instant for ever and ever, an infinite goodness that nothing wearies, that nothing terminates, greater than the sin of the world. This infinite goodness, this eternal faithfulness, this active mercy, is God Who proclaims Himself in the history of His people.

---

[1] *Ps.* 105, 44.
[2] *Ps.* 32, 5.

Nevertheless, all that is still only a preparation. The most profound secrets of divine love have not as yet been revealed. They are veiled by the very images which cover them up while proclaiming them. God is considering a more solemn declaration of His love for humanity and creates a great silence in history to announce it. All the rays of this goodness are but the dawn before the appearance of the sun. God Himself at last appears in the history of the world. The Eternal Word is spoken in time to the ears of mankind. What was hidden from the beginning becomes manifest. He Who was the Invisible becomes the Visible. But now this manifestation prepared from all time and from all eternity, takes on a very special meaning. God unveils in the world the secret of His Being; but it is not an appearance of power, a burst of light, it is a disconcerting manifestation of goodness. Then appeared the benignity of God and His love for men. Lo, the mysterious name that has not yet been spoken, is spoken: He is called Jesus, He is the Savior.

The Redeeming Incarnation is substantially a manifestation of the mercy of God. The fact itself proclaims it enough. God has had pity on our misery. All of Christ's actions repeat it, set it forth in detail in their own way— God appears and it is goodness that acts. We see it and it is a force that heals, a gentleness that pardons. His power appears at the same time as a force that confronts the forces of evil, condemns and conquers them, and is capable of forgiving the immensity of the world's sin. But the focal point of its unfolding is to deliver us from evil by taking upon itself the most grievous consequences of our faults. Behold the Lamb of God, the one Who bears the sin of the world. Thus the whole history of the world acquires its meaning in Christ. The unfolding of sin prepares the unfolding of mercy; or rather the effusion of mercy is present to sin itself and makes use of evil for a new manifestation of love. The sacred history of the world is the mystery of love stronger than hate.

Henceforth everything has been said, because the Word, the very expression of God and, if we may say it, His own face, has appeared in the world. There is no room for any further manifestation of God's love since we have seen Love Itself. We therefore are touching the terminus of the world's history, because its goal has been reached. These are the final times.

And yet, if this manifestation is perfect, since God is entirely there, because of this very adaptation to human conditions, this manifestation of God is capable of being prolonged, even requires prolonging. God is there, manifest, but He expresses Himself in human acts, words, attitudes. No one of them is capable of saying all that must be said. By the very fact of His Incarnation, God has bound Himself in some way, to being conditioned by space and time; His message is addressed to all men and His activity in the world is limited to a particular time and a particular country. Thus, in Christ, there always remains as it were an infinite disproportion between the Divine Love He bears for all, and the few testimonies thereof that He is able to give to some. Even after thirty years of hidden life, after years of service, of concern and of forgiveness, after the Agony, the Scourging, and the Passion, after these excesses which broke His life and opened His heart, there always remain infinite reserves of Love which should have to be manifested in new actions and brought to the knowledge of all men.

It is of this fundamental disproportion between the Divine Love (about which Christ must tell men) and His human actions, that the Church is born. She is born, the Fathers tell us, in the pierced heart of Jesus, as it were of this very breaking of a human heart which exhausted itself to the limit in translating the love of God, and which found itself as it were impotent to do so. This impotence needs a supplement. The love which lives in Jesus needs other hearts to give itself again.

Every man has received a body to show forth in the world the secrets of His soul and to engrave upon it the traits of his action; but He has riches too grand to be expressed in one single visage and to be transmitted in one single life. He needs a bodily supplement, a means of expression and action outside His Body, a Mystical Body over and above His physical Body. This complement of Christ which continues in the world the manifestations of the Divine Love, this Mystical Body which completes His mission in the world, is the Church. It is still Christ, for it is the same manifestation of redemptive mercy, but it is Christ extended to the ends of the world. Just as it is the Divine Love that incarnates Christ in order to show Itself in Him, so is it the Spirit of Christ that raises up the Church, organizes it and gives it life in order to show Itself in her.

These perspectives shed light from above on the direction of the Church's efforts in the world, and the meaning of the mission of the apostle in the Church. It is the Heart of Christ that communicates His life to her and sets her in motion. That is why she is as it were insatiably eager to give to humanity the most pressing testimonials of the Divine Love. She has to go before all misery in order to comfort it, before all lapses to raise them up again, and, finally, in search of all suffering in order to assume it. "The love of Christ impels us." [3]

It is as though the perennial renewals of human misery only provoke her to show the inexhaustible riches of His generosity. Christ still thirsts for new actions and new passions in order to show Himself in His saints. And just as there is no form of human misery over which, through His Church, He does not bend with care, so there is no form of suffering whose burden He, through His Church, has not assumed. That is why the Church, like Christ, ultimately runs up against sin, or rather is fulfilled in the face of sin. It is not a love that meets no obstacle, but a love that no obstacle stops, one she is charged with manifesting. In the face of the ever-increasing immensity of the sin of men, of their ingratitude, their indifference, she shows the inexhaustible longanimity, the fidelity of the Divine Love ever ready to forgive. She organizes in the world a manifestation: the manifestation of mercy.

Let us understand this thoroughly: this is not just any sort of activity that attracts the established Church; it is the order of march that presides at the very founding of the Church. There is an Assembly, there is a Church, precisely for this reason—that there have to be several in order to have mutual love, and therefore in order to show Love in the world. This society lives by interchanges, by services which have a meaning only in showing first of all the communion of persons in the same Charity. These bonds extend beyond all human barriers so that a

---

[3] 2 *Cor.* 5:14.

larger and stronger bond than those of all human group-ings—Divine Love—is manifested.

Thus the internal law of the Church, as it were the distinctive sign of members, is mutual Charity. "By this will all men know that you are my disciples, if you have love for one another." [4]

The very shortcomings that are found in certain members of the Church, far from being an obstacle to the splendor of Charity, are an occasion for it to show itself, and indicate in the human face of the Church what is the proper characteristic of the Divine Love—mercy. "Why are we so sorrowful? It is because we are mortal, fragile and contemptible men, bearing our treasures in clay vessels that clash with one another. But to the contractions that proceed from the flesh, responds the expansiveness that comes from Charity." [5] He who places any accomplishment before that one has not understood the Church. She has not, in the first place, come to bear witness before the world to her success, but to her Charity. Or rather, only when it can be said of her sons: "See how they love one another," only then has the Church succeeded.

2. *Apostolic action, manifestation of Divine Love.*

It is in this Church that the apostle receives his particular vocation as a part of the mission of the whole. He is raised up by Christ, directed by the Spirit to aid the Church, to show forth the Divine Love by his particular insertion into the world. He must be for those who sur-

---

[4] *John* 13:35.
[5] St. Augustine, Sermo 10: *De Verbis Domini.*

round him as a "mystery of God," and so to speak, as a manifestation of His merciful goodness. For it is necessary that the Divine Charity that goes through him pass into all the human fibers of his will and of his heart—it has to be concretized in all the human acts of his devotedness and his concerns; thus is brought to completion in him the mystery of the Incarnation. Looking at it properly, all the human bonds by which he finds himself engaged, bonds of family or of work, of neighborhood or of leisure, and even casual encounters, are destined by God to become bearers of this marvelous message of Divine Charity.

This is at once simplifying and exacting. What light it sheds on the initial orientation of the apostolic soul! First of all, it is not a question of judging others, but of loving them; it is not a matter of propaganda to draw people to the Church as to a society whose strength one is building up, but of a Charity that must be made to shine forth; it is never a question of a party to be defended against other parties, but rather of reconciling in our heart all our human brethren, even if they be divided amongst themselves. Then this love will act not as a constraint but as an appeal, just as God Himself acts, not only respecting liberty, but bringing it about.

But for this to be accomplished, this mystery is exacting. It is not simply a case of giving to others some human marks of goodness and beneficence, but, more precisely, the testimony of a Charity which while remaining human, should appear superhuman, a Charity that tends to pure generosity, attaching itself with a sort of predilection to the poorest, the most abandoned, the most ungrateful. A Charity radically universal for there is no misery in which it can fail to be interested, and which, so to speak, is not within its province; there is no man to whom it has nothing to say. An inexhaustible Charity, for when it has done all that is humanly possible to do, it seems that it has not yet begun. Now the apostle discovers the primary inspiration of all those sentiments which he experiences as if by instinct: it is the Charity of God which is at work in him in order to appear in the world.

If he lets himself be taken up by it, the mystery of Christ and the Church will be accomplished in him. His heart becomes insatiable for good. He would always be wanting to do infinitely more than he is doing; he has the feeling that he has never succeeded in saying what he would like to say, in doing what he ought to do. All misery that has to be helped draws him, his actions are incapable of fulfilling the desires of his heart. That is because the love which bears him up, goes beyond the possibilities of his action. May he suffer therefrom, but may he know that in this he is suffering God, and in this also he resembles his model Christ. Like Him, he has a mission to perform which surpasses human possibilities, a message to transmit that he cannot fully express. But like Him also, his broken heart will, in the end, raise up other apostles who will pass on to the world what he was not able to say. This unity of charity amid diversity of action is the Church herself.

Let him not then be astonished at running into the obstacle of sin, as Christ did. The love he bears the world is a redeeming love. This is what he has to understand if he does not wish to be disconcerted by the difficulty of his mission. It is not by some strange accident that he meets with coldness, disdain or hatred. It is as the law of his development. The love of the apostle must

be shown to the world to be more persevering than indifference, more tenacious than hatred, more powerful
than sin—a love that nothing wearies, that no obstacle
stops, that no refusal breaks, in which the sinner himself finally recognizes a love more than human, the very
Love of God for him. May these occurrences then, however painful they may be, no longer be for the apostle
only a threat of failure to his mission, but a provocation
to realize it fully.

May he go even further—may he accept to bear with
sinners the train of miseries, consequences of sin. The
sufferings of the flesh and the sufferings of the heart, the
distaste for the atmosphere vitiated by evil, the taste of
death. All these things they suffer, let him also suffer
them. May his own insertion into the world, and the
human bonds that are peculiar to him, become for him
the occasion for completing in himself what is wanting
in the Passion of Christ for His Body which is the
Church. That too Christ had to accept in Himself, in
order to show His mercy toward the sinful world. Therefore in him too are verified the words that were spoken
about the Master: "Behold the Lamb of God Who bears
the sins of the world."

He does not do all this alone; he does it in union with
all those who, in all ages and under all skies, have accepted human misery to show the love of God. Because
this action is accomplished in the Church, where all is
put in common by Charity, it is the work of all and belongs entirely to each one. Thus finally, in the Church,
the plan of the Father, the design of Christ, the intimate
desire of the apostle, come to a head—embracing the
world with a total embrace, they express therein in the
measure of the universe, the infinite mercy of God.

3. *The Church, Sacrament of universal salvation.*

Are we to think then that the whole history of the world is but the manifestation of an unceasingly faithful love for an unceasingly rebellious mankind? That the vocation of the Church is to spread abroad a charity unflaggingly offered and unflaggingly refused? That the mission of the apostle is to give forth without respite a call that is never heeded? That the entire activity of God ends in failure and that the first condition of the apostolate is to consent to this law?

Let us admit that, on the experience level, human history remains painfully obscure and particularly undecipherable to us. Sometimes we see a resplendence as from luminous trains that seem to indicate a rising toward salvation; at other times we could rather believe it to be the somber fate of damned masses. It is not on the experience level that we must judge this, but in the light of faith. God has not left us without any light regarding the accomplishment of His design for mankind. As long as the total manifestation of Christ has not taken place, it is not yet in the definitive light; it is in the obscure luminosity of mystery that the signs of the reality to come are given to us. It is not only the face of God and His goodness that appear progressively in the history of the world; it is also the face of humanity and as it were the presentiment of its final destiny, that God gives us to read therein as in a mirror. History is not just a revelation of God manifested to man; it becomes a revelation of man to himself, and these two mysteries march as it were one in front of the other and meet in Christ and in His Church.

A certainty grows in history: not only is God good, but His goodness is efficacious. Not only does God want to save, but He is Savior. It is not a promise—it is a fact. It is sacred history. Human history is a history of salvation. The scope, the proportions of this salvation God reveals gradually in the history of Israel, then in the Church. But His last word has not been spoken. That is why, just as the history of Israel remained mysterious to it insofar as it prepared the Church, likewise the history of the Church remains mysterious to us insofar as it prepares the Kingdom of Heaven. Therefore, if the apostle wants to understand his role and his true efficacy in the world, he has to put himself, with the Church, into her place in the mystery of salvation.

God chose for Himself a people so as to show forth in it His designs for mankind. This entire people has a prophetic role in the world: it announces by its very life the plans of God regarding history. That might have been the manifestation and execution of the gigantic punishment of a recalcitrant people, symbol of the condemnation of a sinful humanity. In effect, it was an unceasing story of salvation, of liberation, of passage from captivity to the Promised Land, from exile to the rediscovered homeland. Amid all the vicissitudes, all the infidelities even, Israel, sometimes punished, always ends up saved. One would think there is always death; and always there is a renewal of life.

The story of Israel in its totality and in all its details, is a story of salvation, but it is not yet the bringing about of salvation; a story of liberation, of conquest of the Promised Land, but not yet the true liberation, the true Promised Land. It is only a temporal image of the eternal salvation. God adapts Himself to the mentality of man who becomes aware of the spiritual only by starting from the sensible, reveals to him His eternal salvation in a temporal history. That is why this history has its reality and also its mystery.

But this image remains strangely disproportionate to the real plan of God for mankind. It both makes it known, and risks obscuring it by what is too carnal and too narrow in it. God keeps for an opportune moment a new manifestation of man's salvation. It is a case of manifesting what He is preparing in two new dimensions.

In extent, the immense plan of God is here revealed. It has to do not merely with keeping safe a chosen people by saving it from the general catastrophe, but of showing forth a plan of universal salvation which goes beyond all boundaries. Or rather it is still a choice, but a choice that extends to humanity. In depth, salvation must in the end appear in its true light: a promise of spiritual blessings, a promise of possessing God Himself, for He is ultimately the true Promised Land of mankind.

The Jewish people, placed, in order to carry out the Divine Plan, in the position of having to raise itself up to the height of these spiritual and universal perspectives, remains in part too carnal and too particularistic to open its heart to this. It becomes attached to the image so as to oppose it to the Truth, and it is its ruination. It breaks with the Divine Plan. It is then that God chooses for Himself a new people to show forth His intentions in the world . . . a chosen people, a people of God, a people saved, but this time in world-wide dimensions—this is the Church. She will be open to the nations: her first claim is that of being universal. She will offer them the enjoyment of divine goods; she is a kingdom that grows in time, but in which one possesses eternal goods. Here the divine design for humanity appears in its true dimensions. It is a design of universal salvation.

Might this at last be the ultimate realization of the merciful plan of God for man? Might this at last be the true Promised Land where we may rest? In one sense, yes, for the Church assures us the true goods which will not be taken from us; she is the final fulfilment of the plan of salvation; she shows its true dimensions. After her there will be nothing greater or more divine. But in a sense also the Church, in her earthly phase, is still only a preparation for the definitive state of mankind. She bears in her bosom the reality of God's people, but what that will be has not yet come to light, or, more exactly, appears only in some precursory signs. The birth of Christ has not yet ended; men are still awaiting it in the world. The Church forms part of this Advent. The Liturgy of the Dawn is accomplished in her, that of the Day has not yet been celebrated. Thus the Church still resembles the Synagogue in that she traces in the world mysterious signs that are projected in the heavens, in order to trace therein the plan of the new humanity. Like Israel, she still has, with regard to the ultimate reality, a prophetic vocation. She announces mankind's lot, she shows it in signs that call for Faith. She herself is this sign of salvation in which we have Faith. But she goes beyond Israel because the sign she delineates is in the very measure of the salvation she announces—especially because it already contains the reality itself of the divine gifts which effectively save the world. The Church is no longer just an image of the salvation prepared for man by God; she is an efficacious sign of the salvation effected by God in humanity—she is the Sacrament of universal salvation.[6]

Such is the mystery of the Church, and such the explanation of her distinctive marks. She bears visibly in herself the invisible dimensions of the Kingdom of Heaven. The Christian recognizes in her the plan of the heavenly City. He sees her beforehand as catholic, reuniting in herself all nations, all races, all classes; one, without any distinction that separates mankind at last united around Christ; apostolic, for this unity transcends the unfolding of time and constitutes mankind's link through the centuries; Roman, because this unity that is accomplished in space goes beyond it, and the unity of the Hierarchic structure manifests visibly the invisible bonds that attach all parts of humanity to a single center acting everywhere—Christ. A single people of the saved, joining all the ages, uniting all peoples around Christ, such is the image of the humanity that is coming, such is the Church.

What she represents, she accomplishes. In pointing something out, she carries it out. The Church effects invisible what she visibly signifies—a universal salvation. Here we are at the heart of her mystery. In a sense, her invisible work does not go beyond her visible action, because she merely carries out its significance. She constitutes a sign of eternal salvation and she accomplishes a universal salvation. That is why she alone saves, because she saves universally. By her very structure she creates in the world a unique and efficacious sign of catholic

---

[6] cf. Liturgy of Holy Saturday: "Deus incommutabilis virtus et lumen aeternum, respice propitius ad totius Ecclesiae, tuae mirabile sacramentum."

salvation. There is no way of being saved outside of the efficacy of this sign, outside the Sacrament of the Church.

But in a sense too, what she accomplishes invisibly surpasses almost to an infinite degree her apparent efficacy. For if the Church, as a sign, represents a universal salvation that goes beyond time and space, as a physical reality she constitutes this sign of universal salvation in the narrow framework of the space she occupies and the time she takes up. In her signification she is universal, and represents a salvation that attains all men beyond the frontiers, and all times beyond the centuries; in her accomplishment, she is particular and constitutes this sign with that part of the human mass and of the unfolding of history that she touches physically. Such is the mystery of the Church—to represent by the action of some men and in the space of a few centuries, the visible sign of a salvation that attains all men and fills all the centuries. And such is the final object of our faith and of our belonging to the Church; we believe that by the powerful mercy of God this sign which He gives to the world, however modest it may be in appearance, really carries out what it signifies—the salvation of mankind.

Thus, through twenty centuries of the Church's life, we see the grace of salvation spread by the Sacraments, as by a single drive across the two thousand years of the history of God's people. What is that in the totality of the world's history? But we know that the people of God represents humanity and accomplishes its mystery, we believe that this sacramental diffusion of grace in the Church represents and effects the impetus of a salvific grace that passes right through mankind in all its temporal breadth. We believe in the Catholic Church, that is, not only do we think that throughout her history, the

Church will, through her Hierarchy, more or less always reach the whole of the known world, but we discover through this fact the mystery of a salvation that is measured by the dimensions of the universe.

The reality of the salvation that the Church effects immensely surpasses what we see of it, while accomplishing exactly what we believe about it through the signs which are given us. Like a woman bearing her child, the Church already bears in herself all mankind and nourishes it with her substance. She finds herself in a state of an internal tendency toward that birthday when the fruit of her womb will appear in the light. She is represented in type by the Virgin of Advent who bears and awaits Jesus, the new humanity. This waiting is a marvelous hope, for the Church knows that the day on which will finally appear the new humanity in the total Christ will be for her at once the perfect fulfilment and marvelous surpassing of all that she has done in the world. The two parables by which Christ enlightens us regarding the development of the Church, that of the grain of mustard and that of the leaven, have as their basis the contrast between the smallness of the point of departure and the incomparable grandeur, the force of penetration of the final result.[7]

God, however, wished to give us a testimony and as a preceding sign in history of this very surpassing of the Church Militant by the Triumphant, and of the Sacrament by the reality, so as to sustain our Faith. It seems that the greatest event in the history of the world was saved in order to prepare us to await this event that completes history. The surpassing of the Synagogue in

---

[7] *Matt.*, 13:31-33.

the Church is for us the symbol and the pledge of the surpassing of the Church of earth in the City of Heaven. It seems that the whole of sacred history was organized only to furnish us, in the relationship of the people of Israel with the Church, with a sort of preparation and type of that final overflowing of the Church into the eternal Kingdom.

Doubtless there is this essential difference, that the Synagogue was to be dispossessed in order to give place to the Church, whereas the Church Militant will not be dethroned, but fulfilled by the Triumphant. Nevertheless, if the leaders of the people were rejected because they attached themselves to the temporal and limited aspect of salvation, the Israel of God, the small faithful remainder, effaces itself before Christ and opens itself to the spiritual benefits He brings to all men. Upon receiving Him, it chants its *"Nunc Dimittis"* and salutes Him: "Light for the Revelation of the Gentiles." In this very effacement it finds its fulfilment. It had at times dreamed of universality, but now saw its desire carried out beyond all it had dreamed. The awaiting is so perfectly fulfilled that it is surpassed. That is the divine way of keeping promises. It is this fulfilment and surpassing of the Israel of God in the Church which is a figure of the definitive accomplishing and superabundant realization of the Church Militant in the Church Triumphant.

Just as Israel saw all its promises fulfilled with a magnificence at once expected and unexpected, so too the Church will one day see carried out the promises contained in the sign of salvation she traces upon the world, in a way both supremely desired and surpassing all desire. Just as the image is accomplished in the universality, foreseen and unforeseen, of the Sacrament, so too the Sacrament will one day be accomplished in the foreseen and unforeseen catholicity of Heaven. The basis of this triple unfolding is the manifestation of the mercy of God in the carrying out of a universal salvation.

That is why the Church can still take up, in her turn, the cries of hope with which the prophetic spirit announced in Israel the universality of salvation. This text of Isaias which she re-reads during the entire Octave of the Epiphany, is still a promise for her, a presentiment, already an exultant vision: "Lift up your eyes, O Jerusalem, look around you. The nations are walking toward your light and the kings toward your nascent brightness. Raise your eyes around you and look: all are gathering and coming to you. Your sons are arriving from afar and your daughters are borne in arms. At this sight you will be radiant, your heart will leap with joy and will be dilated, for to you are flowing the treasures of the sea, the riches of the nations will come to you." [8]

4. *The Church, mystery of election and of grace.*

This transmitting of the promises made to the Synagogue in favor of the Church conceals also another mystery, a mystery that is at the very heart of the vocation of the Church and of her development. She releases into human history and in a visible way, an invisible secret which surpasses all history and without doubt gives the key thereto. It is like a melody that a musician of genius traces and repeats ten times in the course of a symphony, only to make it burst forth at last in the finale in trium-

---

[8] *Is.*, 60, 1-5. Translation is based on the French text not on standard English texts of the Bible.

phant chords, because it causes a re-echoing in the heart
of the total unity and as it were the primary inspiration
of the whole piece. This fundamental rhythm of history
is the preference given by God to that which is small
over that which is great, to that which is poor over that
which is rich, to that which is nothing over that which
seems to be something; a divine melody of history that
finds its ultimate expression on the lips of the Virgin
Mary: "He has put down the mighty from their thrones
and has exalted the lowly. He has filled the hungry with
good things, and the rich he has sent away empty." [9]
From this a series of mysterious reversals, of paradoxical
supplantings of elders by juniors, of the great by the
small, of the fertile by the sterile. But it is not only
Jacob preferred to Esau, Joseph triumphant over his
elders, David the little shepherd chosen to reign, Sara
the sterile called to become the mother of the child of
promise. It is also Mary, the humble Virgin, called to be
the mother of the Messias and of the new humanity, in
preference to all the women of Israel; it is, finally, the
Church, the assembly of the nations, deprived of all
divine promise and of all temporal dominance, and
nevertheless called, she, the last called, in preference to
the Synagogue and to all the powers of the centuries, to
be the Queen of the eternal kingdom, mother of the
humanity to come.

Lastly, beyond all the signs which are given us of it in
its history, it is doubtless the whole of mankind, younger
daughter of God, mysteriously prepared to supplant in
the spiritual universe the firstborn creature—the fallen
Angel Lucifer; it is the Church in her poverty and her

[9] *Luke* 1:51.

weakness, victorious over the forces of hell; and finally, it is Jesus triumphant, carrying humanity along in His glorious Ascension, through the depths of the angelic spheres even to the right hand of the Father.[10]

Why this plan of God? Why does He unceasingly choose that which is the smallest to accomplish that which is the grandest? No doubt in order to manifest more clearly the brilliance of his power, the independence and the gratuitous nature of His mercy: "So then there is question not of him who wills nor of him who runs, but of God showing mercy." [11] Ultimately it is His secret: "O the depth of the riches of the wisdom and of the knowledge of God! How incomprehensible are his judgments and how unsearchable his ways." [12]

With Christ, the entire Church and the soul of the apostle are in sympathy with the design of God of which they are the fortunate beneficiaries. These perspectives shed light from on high on the demands of their activity, the laws of their development and the direction of their destiny: "I praise thee, Father, Lord of heaven and earth, that thou didst hide these things from the wise and prudent, and didst reveal them to little ones. Yes, Father, for such was thy good pleasure." [13]

5. *The Church fights and triumphs relying on God alone.*

The first law of the Church's life is a law of struggle. She does not triumph unless she fights. She is, to begin

---

[10] cf. Danielou, *Mystère de l'Avent*, p. 160.
[11] *Rom.*, 9:16.
[12] *Rom.*, 11:33.
[13] *Matt.*, 11:25

with, a militant Church. It is not independently of the
great spiritual drama of the fall of the Angels that mankind fulfils its destiny. Her whole history is written as
the ultimate vicissitude of this drama that goes beyond
her. She is envied, tempted, tried by hostile spiritual forces
that besiege her and attempt to prevent her from carrying out God's plan. It seems that the permission of God
and the betrayal of men have allowed the powers of evil
to acquire a certain ascendancy over the forces of the
world, which gives them a seemingly redoubtable power.
The Apostle already had remarked it, and the Pontifical
recalls to the Deacons that they are engaging themselves
in a Church forever in a struggle, always in a threatened
situation, not only against flesh and blood but against the
powers of darkness which are acting in the world, against
the evil spirits spread abroad in the air.[14]

This struggle is permitted only to manifest the mercy
of God. His power is shown in making what is weak triumph over what is strong. Thus, it is not on her human
resources that the Church relies in this battle, but on her
very weakness which is the condition of her being open
to grace. She appears at once as the holy Virgin, separated for God from all earthly dealings, but also as the
Spouse, all devoted and accessible by her consent to God's
gift. By that very fact she obtains a mother's fecundity.
The whole history of the Church, all her undertakings,
obey a paradoxical law of despoiling for life. The apostle
will constantly have to take into consideration this sort
of overturning of all human evaluations and all human
tactics when it is a question of the work of Redemption,
failing in which he will understand no part of God's

---

[14] cf. Pontifical of the Deaconate, and *Ephes.*, 6-12.

action in his own life, of the attitudes of the Church in the world and finally of the very mystery of Christ. For it is by the supreme despoiling of the Cross that He, first of all, merited His blessed Resurrection and His glorious Ascension. It is this descent into the depths of human misery which merits for Him the ascent to the right hand of the Father, to which He is drawing humanity in order to fill up the places left empty by the defection of the angels: "He became obedient to death, even to death on a cross. Therefore God also has exalted him and has bestowed upon him the name that is above every name." [15] It is the same law that acts in the Church and draws her through the Cross to triumph.

However, a question we cannot evade imposes itself on the spirit. If God has devised to save the world, why does He delay in doing so? If he wants to make His Church triumph, why does He not grant her to become implanted more widely among all peoples, to penetrate more extensively into the masses? Why is history so often unfavorable to her? Mystery of the maturation of the Church. It is necessary that the sign of salvation she gives to the world be accomplished before being fulfilled. Just as the preparation for the Messias made His absence felt by Israel before overwhelming it with His presence, so too God plants in mankind the desire for universal salvation before making good the expectation. Just as the prophecies delineated the traits of the Messias before His face appeared, in order that the unity of the Divine Plan might be apparent, so also the Sacrament of the Church marks off the dimensions of salvation, in order that its realization might be rooted in the history of the world.

---

[15] *Phil.*, 2, 8.

It is up to God to decide, from the fulness of time, on the hour of the last coming of Christ, just as He decided it for the first one. But even as all the desire and all the effort of Israel and its confidence in the promises hastened the coming of the Messias to which it tended, so the whole expectation and the whole apostolate of the Church are hastening this last coming of Christ with which she, by an intimate law, is mysteriously pregnant.

Such are the meaning and the dynamics of the period of human history in which we live; humanity is saved but it still has to learn of it. The Gospel has to be brought to it. All men are called to salvation, but God wills that they consent to it, and therefore that they know about it. God is preparing the new City in which men will rediscover themselves, but before completing it, He traces a sign of it, through the Church, on the world, a sign to which one must adhere by Faith.

6. *The Church announces the salvation of the world and traces a sign thereof through her Sacraments.*

A dramatic time: though salvation has been acquired for mankind, it remains for each man to take possession of it through Faith. It is through the Church that this is to be done—that is why she is in such haste to carry the Gospel everywhere, for the profession of faith is the most assured sign of the salvation of each man. There is no doubt that God, Who makes use of human means, can do without them. He can present His salvation to whom He pleases, and in the way He pleases. That is why no human forecast can be made on the number of the elect. We cannot affirm it to be great, but neither can we affirm it to be small. Thus does St. Thomas justly conclude: "Finally, it is better to say that God alone knows the number of the elect who are to enter into the eternal happiness." [16]

The revelation given us of it, invites us to think about the ultimate reunion of mankind at once as a choice of the elect in a judgment, and as the manifestation of universality of salvation. The two aspects seem irreconcilable, that is why there remains a mystery; we will see their intimate reconciliation only when the coming of Christ reveals to us the final blossoming of the justice of God in the supreme effusion of His mercy. All we can have a presentiment about, through the signs of it given us in history, is that this coming will be a final manifestation of God in His admirable and ingenious and almighty goodness, and will bring the perfect fulfilment of desires, of action and of the very constitution of the Catholic Church. From now until then, there always remains enough uncertainty for us to act with power, enough assurance to act with confidence.

In this perspective, one understands immediately that the essential work of the Church is to build in herself through her Sacraments, the structure of universal salvation, whose efficacy God, when the time comes, will accomplish. All the time that elapses between the first and the second comings—this time of the Church, is a sacramental time.

7. The victory of the Church is her faith.

Finally, the fundamental disposition that marks this time and sustains the activity of the Church is confi-

---

[16] *Summa Theol.*, Ia, q.23, a. 7.

dence. This type of setback between what we see and what we expect is an appeal to Faith and Hope. This is essential to the work of the Church Militant. God permits precisely that she should not immediately complete her project, that she should even seem to fail sometimes, so as to leave room for this confidence in Him. There, let us understand this, is the very incentive for her action and the secret of her success. It is not so much the power of her efficiency as the intrepidity of her confidence that will bring about in the end the fulfilment of her desire. "No, the king will not be saved by his great power, behold the eyes of the Lord rest on those who fear Him and on those who hope in his mercy." [17] That is why this realization will not be measured by human capabilities, but on the very capabilities of God which she causes to intervene.

In this way are joined the two aspects of the Divine Plan for the Church. It is to the end a manifestation of grace, of gratuitous giving and of mercy. Nevertheless, salvation remains entirely a work of mankind, a work to which it gives all its strength in the Church. But this work is precisely a Sacrament of salvation, which acts through Faith, through confidence in Him Who alone carries out its intent and fulfils its meaning. The most profound attitude of the apostle in the Church is therefore an imperturbable confidence in Him Who, despite all her human weaknesses, through the sign, at once very small and very great, of the mystery of universal salvation that she traces in the world, will respond to her hope by accomplishing it in her. The Spirit repeats in her heart the inspired word: "Do not, therefore, lose your confi-

---

[17] *Ps.* 32. Translation is based on the French text not on standard English texts of the Bible.

dence, which has a great reward. For you have need of patience that, doing the will of God, you may receive the promise: For yet a very little while, and he who is to come, will come, and will not delay." [18]

----

[18] *Hebr.* 10:35.

3

APOSTOLIC LIFE IN THE CHURCH

THESE GRAND perspectives may seem a bit removed from the concrete facts of apostolic action. In reality, they direct it even to its details; they are its very structure. They cannot pretend to form a complete theology of the apostolate, but they suffice to suggest what the intimate dispositions of an apostle in the Church must be.

1. *The sense of the Church.*

The first disposition of the apostle is Faith. He has faith in the Church; that is to say, beyond what he sees of her, a supernatural light discovers for him what she does in the invisible realm. He believes in this plan, he engages himself in this activity, and that is why he confides in the Church. Through the temporal history of the Church, he discovers the instrument of universal salvation; through the modest appearances of the Catholic Sacraments, the glorious expectations of eternal realizations. That is what gives to his activity its meaning and its scope. In the Church, it becomes for him an object of faith.

This action is mysterious; it has repercussions in the invisible. It is what sustains and at the same time orients his courage. He knows that his real influence in the world goes beyond his apparent effectiveness, in order to catch up with the initial drive of his project of universal salvation; but he also knows that his personal activity only obtains its marvelous effulgence through his insertion in the Church. It is that very thing that makes an apostolate of his activity. A man who has a strong personality is quite capable of having an influence on others, and setting up some work or movement in the measure of his genius and of his activity. To reduce the apostolate more or less to this unfolding of personal activity and ingenuity is to misunderstand it entirely. It is a matter of an undertaking of superhuman proportions, a matter of saving the world. A person is capable of doing that only by submitting to the action of God, by entering into His plan, that is to say, by working for the sacrament of universal salvation in the Church. That work and that work alone has an apostolic bearing and efficacy. One becomes an apostle not the day one seeks to exert influence, but the day one puts this influence to the service of the Church. This is not a case of trying to carry out individually a personal effort, or to influence some men. It is a matter of the mystery of the world's salvation. This is accomplished only through the Church. There are no apostles except through the Church and for the Church.

This profound conviction, this supernatural view of the scope of his activity engenders a fundamental disposition in the soul of the apostle: nothing is dearer to him than his attachment to the Church. It is the condition of all that he does and of all that he is. This attachment is manifested and fulfilled by his insertion into the visible structure of the Church, by his active submission to the Hierarchy. It is a matter of giving the world the efficacious sign of universal salvation. This sign cannot be formed except in dependence upon the Hierarchy. Outside of this hierarchical order, in fact, there is no longer either visible unity or catholicity; there is no longer any Sacrament of salvation, there is no longer any Church, there are no longer any apostles. Hierarchical submission is therefore the very fabric of apostolic action, a fact which constitutes its mystery and confers upon it its supernatural effectiveness in the plan of God. It is at the price of this obedience and of this confidence that God makes use of our activity to accomplish His designs. For apostolic effort, it is not a simple matter of discipline, of coordination of efforts; it is a matter of existence. It does not permit the apostle to operate in a better way—it permits him simply to act as an apostle. It does not grant him to be better; it grants him to be.

He who would seek to carry out personal plans of salvation for a milieu or a social class apart from hierarchical submission, does so because he has not understood what the apostolate is. He fails to recognize its mystery. He has fallen back to the level of a natural view regarding the efficacy of his action. Perhaps he believes he operates more grandly or more capably, but he does less, does nothing, because he is acting humanly instead of divinely. He risks realizing too late, to his detriment, that "the foolishness of God is wiser than the wisdom of men."[1]

---

[1] 1 Cor. 1:25.

This sense of the Church orients apostolic aspirations. It is not a matter of wishing and promoting the success of our work, of our movement, of our parish and thereby of ourselves. It is a matter of entering into the plans of the Church and of promoting her success. Sometimes the apostle will have to sacrifice all actual success in preparing for the future success of the Church. A particular missionary in a Moslem country, for example, is assured of spending all his life without any appreciable results on the surface; he does not even wish to obtain such immediate success as would compromise the future. By this very renunciation he is fully an apostle. He is working for the Church.

This manner of seeing things permits a more lively experiencing of the solidarity that binds apostles in the common work. No one can undertake anything alone; it is the work of men linked together, and, so to speak, of their bond itself; the work of a continuity, of an organism. No one in the organism can be disregarded, each one is of service to all for the common effort. All those who, within the Church, concur in one way or another in maintaining the Hierarchy and the sacramental order, concur by that very fact in the common salvation. Also, the law of apostolic success is not to seek to reap and count the fruits of personal success: "There is one who sows and another who reaps, but all will rejoice in the work accomplished together." [2]

This insertion in the Church not only touches our exterior activity, but our whole spiritual life. We live in the Church and for her even to our most intimate prayers and sacrifices. We accept the fact that the rhythm of our

---

[2] *John* 4:36-37. Translation is based on the French text not on any standard English texts.

prayer and of our penance pass through her structures, as well as those of our own action. But that is not a constraint for the Christian, because his vocation calls him to live in the Church, so that by this very insertion he discovers that for which he is made. In the Church and in the Church alone his prayer reaches its fulness in the liturgical mystery; his suffering finds its meaning in rejoining that of the Mystical Body, just as his action ends by being inserted into a catholic structure. It is there that he lives, that he breathes and fulfills himself completely. And without doubt that is not accomplished without renouncing his tastes and his particular aims, but this very submission, by detaching prayer and action from their own caprice, paradoxically permits their full liberty in the pure gift of self to the designs of the Father.

2. *The sacramental sense.*

Another practical consequence of these general perspectives is the importance of the sacramental order. The principal object of apostolic labor is to form in the world the Sacrament of universal salvation. This Sacrament is constituted by the hierarchic structure of the Church, and by the insertion of the faithful of all lands into this hierarchic organization. This insertion is visibly effected by the Sacraments. One could scarcely minimize without error, the importance of the sacramental order in apostolic work. The latter tends essentially to bring people to the Sacraments in order to form the Sacrament which is the Church.

This orientation has a two-fold value. First of all, it has, fundamentally, a social value. Salvation operates socially by the constitution of this sign of catholic salvation which is the Church. To work at it through the association of new elements, is to give one's action a universal scope, the only one that responds to the exigencies of the Christian apostolate.

The sacramental life has moreover a personal importance for the salvation of those whom we attract. Their salvation is only assured by their faith in the saving plan that God carries out in the Church, by a certain attachment to her mystery. No doubt this attachment may for certain people consist in a desire that is authentically supernatural, though invisible and at times implicit. It remains that, if it is sincere, it tends to be expressed in exterior acts as soon as they become possible. That is why the practice of the Sacraments remains the most certain sign of belonging to the Church and of personal insertion into the mystery of salvation.

Of course, because it is not as yet the reality itself of salvation but a sign that prepares for it, we cannot say that he who practices is by that very fact assured of being saved. By the same token he is not on the same footing as he who does not practice; for the reception of the Sacraments is the normally efficacious sign of grace. So that although we might always have apprehensions for the salvation of those who do practice, and hopes for the salvation of those who do not practice, we can say that only those who receive the Sacraments are visibly on that path which leads to salvation for themselves, and in the structure which is bringing about the salvation of the world. This conviction suffices to recall continually to the apostle that the basis of his action is oriented to the participation of all those he reaches in the sacramental mysteries within the Church.

But, obviously, he will recall at the same time that

these rites do not have a magical power and demand on the part of those who approach them a lively faith which makes them grasp their meaning, lacking which these acts would lose their religious value and would become formalism or superstition. That is why, if he is urged to lead to the Sacraments, he is at the same time discreet, and at times will know how to be severe so as to admit to them only those who approach them in a religious spirit. But that in itself is a springboard for his action. He tends precisely to spread faith in Christ, not to stop there and excuse people from entrance into the Church and from the practice of the Sacraments, but to prepare for it. While the preparation might be long, it remains always bent on this goal. The important thing is to put each thing in its place: not faith without religious practice, nor practice without faith, but faith in order to prepare for the sacramental life.

This requires not only an exterior attitude, but inspires an interior disposition which is as the very atmosphere of all apostolic life. It is a matter of avoiding two excesses. On the one hand we have to avoid sadness and the almost despairing anxiety of the man who judges his action's result only by the deceptive statistics of sacramental practice. But we must also avoid the deceitful security and lazy assurance of the man who would believe that salvation is given just as well outside the Sacraments and without visible insertion into the Church. The apostle will find the balance between these two attitudes, one of which leads to excessive rigor and to discouragement, the other to excessive ease and to presumption, by replacing his activity in the whole of the Church's mystery. He will be all the more ardent in promoting the sacramental life, the more he knows that not only is this contact with the Sacraments the surest gauge of the salvation of those who approach them, but that it also bears invisible fruit for all mankind. His concern for sacramental activity is not founded on the despair of saving those who escape him, but on the hope of enclosing them in the solid meshes of this salutary net. Perhaps it is with a small flock that he celebrates the Divine Liturgy, but he offers himself with them, in the Church, and offers Christ for the salvation of the entire world, while at the same time thinking of all those who are not present.

3. *The missionary spirit.*

In these perspectives one grasps at once the necessity of the missionary spirit, and its precise meaning. It is essential for the Church to establish a sign of salvation that might visibly reach all parts of known humanity, in order to reach invisibly the unknown depths. Since St. Paul, she tends unceasingly to perfect catholicity, for she knows that when the world is, in its totality, enclosed within the salutary net of the Sacraments, then God, fulfilling the mysterious signification of this sign, will accomplish the unity of the salvation prepared for all people. It is then the whole Church which by her very constitution, is working constantly to reach the entire world. It is not just certain of her members who specialize in this work of penetration, it is all her members and all her activities that tend thereto. It is impossible to be a Christian if at the same time one is not a missionary.

This allows us to understand more exactly the orientation of this missionary labor. It is not a matter so much of individually reaching all men, as it is of establishing over the whole surface of the globe and in all the depths of humanity, the visible, hierarchic and sacramental structure of the Church, the efficacious sign of universal salvation. As Fr. Charles said, the goal of the missions is "to implant the Church."

4. *The sense of poverty as the disengagement from human supports.*

This undertaking is gigantic, or more exactly, super-human. That must be emphasized so as not to let the supernatural character of the Church's action be degraded in practice. This action is a struggle and a combat; it is a conquest and the founding of a Kingdom. But this Kingdom is not to be confounded with any political party, any civil society; that is why it disconcerts them all. It does not enter into their field. The apostle who would simply place himself at the service of a party or of a class or of an activity, would be permitting a degradation of the meaning of his message and would be contributing to a failure to recognize the face of the Church. The Church may indeed bring to all peoples the goods of civilization, she may indeed tend to relieve the miseries of all classes, she may seek to bring a remedy to all social disorders, yet the good things which she brings are transcendent with respect to all these human advantages. She makes use of all human advances, but she is not at their service; she obtains them, as it were, to boot—but she aims higher. That is why the militant who would want to reduce his activity to promoting a better social organization or to spreading a temporal beneficence without referring it all to the restoration of the Church by faith in Christ and the sacramental life, would no longer be doing apostolic work.

Finally, it is necessary to add that if the goal of the Church is not to install a new political order nor to procure temporal goods, but to establish the Kingdom of God in which one enjoys eternal goods, in order to obtain this supernatural end she can only use supernatural means. It is not a human project that she carries out with human forces. Her law of life is to carry out something superhuman while sloughing off human means. Her poverty is her strength, for it is what causes the power of God to burst forth in her. That does not mean that the Church cannot employ for her action the riches and the resources of this world, all the inventions of modern techniques, and the currents of history. But, differently than a human undertaking that counts on these forces for its accomplishment, the Church does not count on them, she uses them as though not using them. At the very moment when she does make use of them, she considers all the riches of this world as poverty in view of the goal to be obtained, all its forces as impotence. But this poverty and this weakness do not discourage her, for they assure her of the help of God. Appearing thus stripped and as it were unarmed in the face of the enormous powers of this world does not frighten her, for her shield is invisible; it is the power of God. That is why there will always be in the Church the two-fold, balanced manifestation of a universal use of the resources of human history in the service of the Kingdom, and of a constant disengagement from all human means, so that her transcendence might indeed appear. Each apostle, each religious family, will have to integrate these two aspects. According as he will be called upon to manifest one or the other in particular, his spirituality will have a particular orientation. Poverty is for all; some will insist on poverty in usage, others on poverty in being deprived. It remains that the apostle will never expect the success of his apostolate from a change of political regime, nor from any human support, but from God alone. That will keep him from many disillusionments and also many deviations and compromises.

5. *The sense of humility, confidence in the Divine help.*

We must go further: not only does the apostle not count on the resources of the human powers of this world to succeed, he does not even count on his personal resources. It is this which, practically, constitutes the supernatural pace of his action. In human action there is a project being developed, methods being discovered to carry it out, energy set in motion to bring it to completion. It is the harmonious unfolding of this goal, of this drive and of this repose that is the support and the joy of action. On the supernatural level, that is not all destroyed, for grace does not suppress nature, but surpasses it. If the apostle displays all his ingenuity and puts to work all his forces, it is not so much in the manner of a wealth which God needs as it is of a poverty which God is willing to use for a transcendent goal. The incentive of his efficacy is no longer in himself but in God; or more exactly in the gift, stirred up by grace, that he makes to God of his own deficiency so as to provoke the effusion of His mercy. That is why apostolic activity conceals a mystery from the eyes of men and of the apostle himself.

There is always a disproportion between what he does and what he hopes for. His views and his calculations always surpass his resources. He counts on God. His life is a project that surpasses his action. It is precisely this transcendence of his true vocation, of what he is called to do in this world, this transcendence of his destiny with regard to his functions, which allows him a sort of spiritual independence toward the places he occupies and the activities he engages in. He is not diminished by a modest job, for he is able to have a great life, a great influence, in small tasks. He is not puffed up by important concerns, for as great as his human work might be, it is but a drop of water offered for the immensity of the goals he pursues.

His heart is always above what he is doing. His center is elsewhere, or rather at once inside and beyond him. His influence progresses not so much through vaster enterprises as through a deepening toward this intimate center, immanent and transcending all action, where he offers all that he does and all that he suffers as an appeal to grace. That is why the progress of apostolic action lies not so much in a more and more powerful and rapid unfolding of human methods, as in a more and more total giving, remitting and bending of all his resources to the divine proceedings, toward the putting into operation of the infinitely small by the infinitely great. At its completion the activity tends to be less of an agitation and more of an effulgence. It unites itself more to the source, it resembles more the peaceful and calm activity of God, it is on the march, through time, toward eternal life.

6. *The sense of obedience, mark of faith.*

But this progressive surpassing of too-human assurances is not done without us. It is necessary that we have the occasion of manifesting in acts this supernatural view which assures the efficacy of the undertaking before God by giving more value to the giving than to the efficiency. It is certainly one of the goals of hierarchic submission to thus purify our action by making it less the realization of our personal plans than the total offering of ourselves to the will of God represented by our superiors. That is why the apostle who truly has the sense of the properly supernatural dynamism of his action prefers small tasks in obedience to great performed apart from it.

7. *The sense of the contemplative life.*

This profound law of the supernatural efficacy of the apostolate, which does not lean on human means but on the grace of God, is as it were inscribed in the very structure of the Church by the contemplative state. There is something in the apostolate that escapes someone who has no understanding of the contemplative life. The contemplatives are not idle members of the Church. They are not without influence, but visibly recall to everyone, by stripping themselves of exterior activities, that the most intimate secret of the apostolate is offering. By their total renunciation of the joys of action they communicate to the apostles the strength for the disentanglements necessary to preserve their activity in its supernatural purity. By their example, they teach them not to count too heavily on human powers, not even on their own strength. By their state of life, they are witnesses to the final stage where the apostolate will be accomplished as a pure radiating of the intimacy of love with God. Like the virgins on the level of love, they are, on the action level, precursors of eternity.

On the other hand, by the concrete examples of their

devotedness, the apostles unceasingly remind the contemplatives of the real demands of the gift of self. They help them to maintain the mobility of a vocation which would fall below action if it were only a flight from obligations and a search for tranquillity, and which can only be carried out by surpassing action in generosity on the path of renunciation. Thus, these two states are brought to completion in the Church, and manifest the two complementary and, in appearance, contradictory aspects of apostolic action: that it sets into operation all human resources, but ultimately relies only on God.

8. *The sense of the Cross.*

Besides, no matter what might be the vocation to which one is called, one will not get away from the necessity of renouncing the natural taste for action, personal projects and successes. One will not avoid the mystery of the Cross. In this light, far from fleeing it, we will welcome it as the means par excellence of realizing the greatest ambitions. Herein is accomplished the paradox of supernatural action; the renunciation of all human support and all private success, opens the way to the divine force that reaches the universal. The sense of the Cross joins the missionary spirit. In destitution and immobility, which consummate the gift of self, the crucified man acts on the universe and obtains all riches in the measure of the gift of God. Torn from all earthly support, he rests on God's strength; that is why his influence reaches the world and finally fulfills the roots of his missionary desire in a fruit of catholic redemption: "I, if I be lifted up from the earth, will draw all things to myself." [3]

---

[3] *John* 12:32.

9. *The sense of action in the Church as an act of faith in the fidelity of God.*

There is then an incessant effort to be made in apostolic action, in order to maintain it on its true level. We are labored by immense desires and are gripped by the sorrowful experience of our personal impotence and of the apparent impotence of the Church to fulfill them. On whom then to steady ourselves since all human support fails us? Who will fill the abyss between our projects and their fulfilment? Who will give our action its spirit and its joy? God alone. If we are stronger than all the powers of this world and of hell leagued against us, it is because our weakness leans on God by faith: "This is the victory that overcomes the world, our Faith." [4]

Is this to say that we are no longer to act? On the contrary—understanding all the while that what constitutes the supernatural worth of action is precisely that it is a lived manifestation of confidence. Action is hope, not only in words but in acts. It is an intrepid hope, by which man really commits his property and his being on God's word. If we may thus express ourselves, he stakes his life itself in a gamble on God's fidelity . . . total risk in total security. It is this indeed which pleases God and which, in short, He rewards. The world will have to recognize at last that all these fools were right!

Precisely because it is apostolic confidence which is supremely efficacious in the world, God is pleased to demand it. One would say that all His action on the Church and in His saints only tends to deepen it. Human means escape them; at times the very work done seems to crum-

---

[4] *John* 5:4.

ble; over and above all failures and all defections, they remain assured of the fidelity of God. It suffices for them. In total darkness they proclaim their imperturbable confidence. One might say that God is pleased to test it, to provoke it, to see just how far it will go. They enter into this divine game, so to speak; it is a challenge—they take it up. They are beyond confusion.

At this price, the apostle discovers a secret of peace and of supernatural assurance. There is a balance of action between a tension too rigid because too human, and a discouraged relaxation, which can only be found through this confidence in God. This higher view of the manner of the apostolate's effectiveness permits us to accept without friction, submission to the orders of superiors and harmony with those who work at the same level, even at the cost of certain constraints. The sacrifices are finally consented to without breaking up the drive toward the goals pursued, because in this perspective, they too lead to the goal.

This light enlightens our adherence to the Church. In her too, our confidence is put to the test. To put it more accurately, she is wholly, through the Sacrament of salvation she effects, an immense act of confidence which awaits its fulfilment by God. Our faith and our action ratify this confidence of the Church. God purifies it in the course of the centuries. It seems that all the powers of this world are mobilized in order to try her. But her hope comes out of it strengthened. Her victory in time over each of her particular enemies is for her only a new image and a pledge of her ultimate victory over the enemy of the human race. She leans on the Faithful One. Also, just as the difficulties which sometimes hobble the success of action, do not leave us discouraged, so too the persecutions that beat down upon the Church and at times leave her weakened, do not disturb us in our attachment. We know that God makes use of this weakness, that He makes it the instrument of His strength.

It is good for us to become aware of it in these times when the Church is attacked and threatened from so many sides; it is not only an attachment that is resigned despite her failures; it is a loving attachment because of the very injuries done to our mother and the marks which remain on her from them, and which perhaps disfigure her, but through which her children still recognize her. In her, we are happy to follow Jesus, from the Pretorium to Calvary.

Much more, our faith has given us a presentiment that these very sufferings of the Church are preparing and hastening her triumph. Has it not been foreseen? "And you therefore have sorrow now; but I will see you again, and your heart shall rejoice, and your joy no one shall take from you." [5] There is more or less an extreme point of despoiling and of humiliation, where confidence asserts itself in a manner so pure and so tearing that it reaches the Heart of the Father and brings about the decisive intervention of His Mercy. It is the final cry of Jesus on the Cross. It is the summit of every apostolic life when action is achieved in passion. It is the term, too, of the whole life of the Church.

Her history obeys, it seems, a double rhythm of development and of tearing away. These two movements lead her to her triumphant goal. They are opposed only in appearance. Her very growth prepares her in the measure of the Cross God destines for her. It is when she has

_____

[5] *John* 16:22.

been extended over the whole world that she will be able to be crucified on the whole world and that she will finally save all of it. Ultimately, God only pursued this intensity of confidence purified by trial in order to let people see in the end, how He is able to reward it. He seems to ask a great deal, but He knows it is nothing, a laughable effort of some moments, compared to the immense blessings and the eternal joys that His faithfulness is preparing for those who trust in Him.

God, nevertheless, throughout creation and history, gives us some image of it. The immense fecundity of all nature, which swells it with riches each new springtime, is but a starting point allowing a glimpse of the admirable fecundity of the saint who himself, also transmits life in mysterious generations in this Promised Land of which the first is but a symbol, for the springtime of eternity: "The just man shall flourish like the palm-tree, he shall grow like the cedar of Lebanon." [6] More than the best wheat, he yields forty, sixty and hundred to one: a fabulous harvest, still, an inadequate image. This natural multiplication is tiny in comparison with the promises of God; He needs the sand of the sea and the innumerable army of the stars in the sky; He needs, in history, all the posterity of Abraham, to give a rough estimate of His generosity toward those who have left all in faith: "I will make thy posterity as numerous as the sands of the sea. Look in the heavens, count the stars if you can, it is thus that thy descendants will be." [7] Admirable promises these, which the Gospel goes on to apply to those who, to follow Christ, left everything for Him; it is merely revealing the unsuspected scope thereof. What the apos-

---

[6] *Ps.* 91:13.
[7] *Gen.* 13:16; 15:5; 22:17.

tles are to give is not mere carnal life, for the purpose of introducing on this earth a multitude of descendants; it is eternal life, for the purpose of introducing into heaven multitudes of the elect: "You shall also sit . . . judging the twelve tribes of Israel." [8] An astonishing prospect, of which the jurisdiction found in the Church already gives us a sacramental sign which sustains our waiting. But when the reality of the ultimate outpouring of the Mercy of God shall appear, it will indeed be necessary to convince ourselves that it surpasses all expectation.

10. *The sense of the Priesthood in the Church.*

Ultimately, it is this final triumph that God is preparing through all of this. He asks so much only in order to be eternally justified in giving so much. He made the world and directed history only in order to evoke the total confidence of His saints and to fulfill their desires, but He raises up saints only in order to fill the world, through them, with His divine joy . . . a two-fold revelation of mercy. He accepts this representation in the gift of all through one alone—a sacerdotal character of the apostolate which is inscribed in the very structure of the Church. Once and for all, Christ is chosen as the unique priest, of Whom all is demanded even to the death of the Cross, because all is to be given over to Him for eternal life.

The Church also, in Christ, is sacerdotal; she is chosen in the world to be separated, offered, immolated, because God wants to fill her with His blessings for all, to grant her to keep in herself the riches of the nations for

---

[8] *Matt.,* 19:28.

eternity. The apostle, too, sees the sacerdotal mystery accomplished in himself. He contemplates the efficacious sign of it in the priest consecrated by the Church, of whom God demands visibly his whole life, in order that he might distribute Christ sacramentally to all men. He too, by reason of His Baptism and his Confirmation, is drawn into this sacerdotal activity in the Church, and he knows that, if God asks more of him in her, it is to give him more, not only for himself, for a multitude of others too. And that is why he knows that this final accomplishing of his apostolate will respond not only to the human efficacy of his action, but to the generosity of God Who employs it; beyond all the deceptions of time, it will catch up to the immensity of his desire in eternity, God put it there at the beginning only in order to fulfill it in the end.

If he is aware of the riches which are destined for him, the apostle's adherence to the Church will no longer be simply resigned, nor even just loving, but enthusiastic. This atmosphere of total confidence, of complete submission to all the promptings of the Church, of participation in all the pulsations of her life, in her sufferings and in her hopes, such is the supernatural climate in which the apostolic soul develops. Through all trials, its action unfolds with strength and peace, in joy because it comes from God, because it is going to God and reposes in God. Who will keep it from attaining its goal? "If God is for us, who is against us?" [9]

---

[9] *Rom.* 8, 31.

4

APOSTOLIC PURIFICATIONS

WE ARE FAMILIAR with the famous analyses by which Saint John of the Cross has pointed out the progress of contemplation. He discovers in the night of the senses and the night of the spirit, a sort of internal law of the contemplative life which leads it, by the sheer rhythm of its normal development, unto a stripping away of everything, for the perfect purity of love. Recently, two authors, beginning from altogether different viewpoints, have analyzed the progress of human love. One, Dr. Allendy,[1] looks at it as a physician and a psychoanalyst; the other, Jean Guitton,[2] studies it as a psychologist and metaphysician. The latter is a Christian, the other is not. Nevertheless, on one point at least, they come to the same conclusion: human love is subject to an internal law of development which has to set forth, progressively, by the very action of psychological evolution, its most disinterested aspect, which both call "the oblative forces of love." Thus love, even in its most carnal form of sexual

---

[1] Dr. Allendy, *L'Amour*, Paris, Denoel.
[2] Jean Guitton, *Essai sur l'amour humain*, Paris, Aubier.

love, tends by its own rhythm of growth to purify itself, and, may we say, to set forth its essence, which is the gift of self. Its very life makes it rise up and sing out more and more purely as love. The life of love is to become pure love.

We would like to show here that it is the same in another domain, that of the apostolic life and of that love which spends itself in action. The life of the apostle and his activities are subject, by very reason of their human growth, their psychological development and the rhythm of their action, to some profound transformations. A person does not approach action with the same courage at sixteen years and at sixty. That is a fact we must recognize, a law we cannot get away from. At first glance, this psychological transformation might seem without importance from the viewpoint of the spiritual life. One could even believe that it represents little more than a sort of progressive relapse of the energies of action, so lively at the beginning of the apostolic life, and at times so weakened at the end of it.

From this point of view, the ideal thing would be to maintain, all of one's life, the enthusiasm of a twenty-year old. But how quickly that is shown to be unrealizable! It would be going contrary to psychological laws that are imposed on us and over which we have no control. It comes about then, that we become discouraged and end up considering a relapse fatal and spiritual progress impossible in the life of the apostolate, for not having seen, perhaps, of what the latter must consist. We would end up believing that from this side of the mountain, it is not possible to go all the way to the top, perhaps only because we have not discovered the road that leads up to the summit. There is nothing more danger-

ous for the apostle and for his action itself, than this sort
of discouragement that threatens to take possession of
him in the middle of his life, in this noontime when the
limitations of human forces show up, when their decline becomes imminent and when confusion between
the possibilities of man and the gifts of God risks bringing about the collapse of the ideal as well as the failure
of dreams.

It is, therefore, a matter here of showing, after a rapid
analysis of the different psychological stages of the apostolic life, that this very development of the phases of
human activity normally calls for an increase and a grad-
ual purification of our supernatural life. A purely human
outlook would make us see a rise followed by a relapse,
a development of action and of radiance, followed by a
cutting back and an ageing, youth followed by decrepi-
tude. A supernatural outlook will show us that through
this rhythm of human activity, God calls us to a con-
tinual progress, unceasingly accelerated, not only in love,
but in action itself. But this progress is supernatural. It
tends to set off the supernatural character of apostolic
activity, in an ever-purer way. Also, it is from a viewpoint
of faith that we have to discover and accept it, and it is
in accepting it that we discover it. That does not come
about of itself; it is an effort and an ascension sustained
by grace.

A person has no comprehension of the progress of the
contemplative life until he has grasped the fact that
through all weaknesses and aridities, God calls the soul
to a total giving and to a purer love in which He secretly
reveals Himself, so that the void consented to by love
becomes the supreme possession of the All. One has no
understanding of conjugal life until he has realized that,

through all its phases, from betrothal to widowhood, it bursts human egoism, eliminates the interested aspects of love, in order to bring one to the purer giving of self, for which is opened the way to a more spiritual coming together that nothing can again affect, with the result that separation itself completes and purifies intimacy. Likewise, finally, one does not understand the progress of the apostolic life until he has accepted, through all the phases of human life, through all successes and failures, the invitation of the Father to give himself more purely and to abandon himself more completely, in order to become in His hands, the instrument of the world's salvation, so that the very suffering of the apostle becomes his supreme shining forth.

I. PSYCHOLOGICAL STAGES OF AN APOSTOLIC LIFE

We do not here have to retrace the entire moral and religious evolution from earliest infancy to adult age. That has already been done. We should like to show how, in the different ages of life, from adolescence to old age, the apostolic ideal is envisaged and concretely lived. Doubtless, we will only be able to uncover some rather general characteristics. It would be quite impossible to go into details, which are individual and infinitely diverse. But we think that the general outline of development which comes to light at the completion of these analyses, can apply to the majority of cases, and that the exceptions themselves, wherein the normal tempo is accelerated and at times transformed, will be able to make use of the spiritual trends that are deduced from habitual progression, in order to grasp their proper destiny.

1. *Adolescence.*

Very young children can already have apostolic initiatives that are at times astonishing. A certain orientation of devotedness, an authentic sacerdotal or missionary vocation, can be born in the heart of a little one, like a wonderful and fragile flower in the first days of spring. But the formed and definitive plan of consecrating oneself to giving Christ to one's brethren, normally asserts itself during the course of adolescence, between thirteen and seventeen years of age.[3] It is at that moment that the personl project is uncovered, tried, and finally, made definite. That which forms the apostle is precisely that, in a supernatural light and under the influence of God, a young man or a young girl is unable to think of him or herself without seeing and wanting him or herself in the service of others in order to give them Christ. This presents itself in a thousand outward forms, sacerdotal vocation or vocation of lay militant, but at bottom there is this that is common: "My personal progress is to be the one who gives himself for Christ." Humanly, the adolescent chooses his vocation, chooses to be an apostle. Basically, it is God Who chooses him, out of love for him and love for them. He is moved by God and accepts this motion toward others; he is sent; he will be an apostle.

These easy-going formulas give a very faint idea of what this apostolic vocation can concretely be. In fact, it is almost always in the middle of a difficult struggle against other, more palpable attractions, that it presents

---

[3] cf. Loret, A *quel âge se décident les vocations?* in Recrutement sacerdotal, Jan. 1949. "The childhood vocation, without being disdained, must be considered a provisional attitude." (Translation mine)

itself. It is a choice, as diverse as environments and persons are diverse, between a certain project of human success, of temporal enjoyments, and the ideal of the only success that counts, saving men for eternity, and of the only joy that lasts, loving Christ and making Him loved. It is a preference given to the pursuit of this Kingdom of Heaven whose spiritual goods are only foreseen, over all the fleshly goods that surround us, attract us and flatter us. It is a victory of the spirit over the passions, an accepted inrushing of supernatural light which illumines for us the real blessings, a victorious impulse of love, a total confidence placed in Jesus Christ Who takes possession of this life in order to accomplish in it and through it, His designs of salvation.

One might readily characterize the attitude of this period of life toward future activities in a few words: it is the age of *the ideal, dreamed of and consented to*. In order that this formula might be valid, we would have to remove from the word dream whatever is pejorative about it. We should not believe that adolescence necessarily shuts itself up in a vain revery, separated from reality, though that might be a pitfall that awaits it. What characterizes this period is first of all, the conception of the ideal, the anticipation, in a certain intimate plan, of life's trends. A plan at once personal and social, a looking ahead to what one has to be and what one wants to do. Personality is defined, and already formed, in this sketch of the future.

Of course, the elements thereof are drawn from reality. We might easily discern the influence of the family environment, the attraction of great examples encountered, the call of the needs of the times. All that is put into operation by grace, which discovers its supernatural meaning. But this plan which takes possession of real elements, fashions them in its likeness and idealizes them. It is the privilege of this age not to be too narrowly determined as yet by the mold of concrete circumstances. It is already able to foresee all its possibilities, without having to choose among them. It has not had to prune the branches of desire in order to obtain the fruits of realization. It is above all its privilege to fashion the future. The plasticity of the future enables it to conceive it in its own way, and to conceive itself, in this future, in a beautiful way. Difficulties are of course foreseen, but these are imagined more than confronted.

The elements drawn from reality serve to give the value of something possible to that which the pressure of life and of grace bring to life. This imagined and ideal presentiment of what one wishes to do has not yet gone into the mold of the concrete. In this, the plan resembles a dream. It is that which often gives this age a somewhat presumptuous assurance with respect to the generations that have preceded it. It instinctively compares its ideals to their accomplishments. That makes it severe. If only it would be allowed to act and to command! It feels itself ready to transform everything. Certain people are shocked by these rather youthful words . . . But it is on the whole a good thing that this is so. This role of idealizing the plan of life and action renders it more attractive to the feelings.

It is also the age of great enthusiasms. We must not make fun of them. In the lively and still subtle fire of these ardent desires the will is going to ignite and flare up. We must not turn aside from the law of the human being which wants the True to pass through the senses in order to reach the intellect, and the Good through the feelings in order to make the will fruitful. Here in fact, through these excitements of youth, great decisions are made. It is the age of total giving and of heroism. Through these images and these dreams, the call of God is heard and accepted. In the generous plans of the adolescent, the child decides to be a dedicated person. The apostolic ideal takes on the characteristics which give it its proper content and delineate its personal form. Long dreamed of, slowly matured, here it is at last definitively consented to. The apostle is ready for the departure.

2. *The young man.*

This starting on the way is truly a stage of the apostolic life. This penetration of the ideal caught sight of and consented to, in reality presupposes the putting into operation of new faculties. The willed ideal becomes *the pledged ideal.* The plan becomes a reality. Whether it be to begin immediately the action of a militant, or to undertake the formation which prepares the apostle, it is necessary at this point to surmount the opposition of the environment and the inertia of the old man. Such entrance into the period of accomplishing is a trial for the apostolic ideal. Some stumble right from the first step. Like those deceptive vehicles whose motor races as long as they are out of gear, but dies out as soon as one wants to start, we see some young people, capable of vast projects and of generous words, but incapable of taking one step. One enters the seminary with enthusiasm, but comes out a few days later, disenchanted; another, who applauds the program of some movement, is unable to make any effort on its behalf.

At times, there is a crisis and it seems that there is retrogression. The initial excitement subsides. A new rhythm imposes itself which is not that of the feelings but of the will. It is necessary that the impetuosity of desires pass over into the regular and ordinary pace of humble daily reality. It is necessary to use the energy that a splendid plan generates to carry out very small things.

What a strange use God makes of these lively forces. In all this we have to understand, in a supernatural light, that this change of conditions is progress. If the initial drive passes into such a narrow channel, it is in order to give it more strength. And if the desire for action is expressed in such small accomplishments, it is for an increase of love. Progress, because there is accomplishment; for it is here that the apostolate begins. It is in this lived obedience, in this active love, in this confronting of difficulty that it consists. It is not he who says "Yes, yes" who is the apostle, but he who does the will of the Father in the Church for the salvation of the world. The first difficulties and suffering encountered are an occasion of exercising and increasing true love. There is more charity in accepting one hour of work in reality, than ten years in imagination. It is progress, too, because this becomes the sign that what is sought is not a plan of personal ambition and of self-promotion, but a plan of submission to the will of the Father. By this very smallness, we enter into evangelical greatness.

Such is the condition of the young man—a transitory condition. He feels it and he is eager to come to that adult age of full realization for which he is made; for, throughout these difficulties, his primal project remains intact. The partly-seen ideal is always desired. Only it will take longer than he thought. In the course of his difficult way he is sustained by the great desires he is pursuing. He is straining toward the accomplishment of this plan which he bears in him ever since the decisive days of his adolescence, no part of which he has denied. His action has all the more gusto according as his few successes are for him already the foretaste and the precursory sign of successes to come, whereas his failures in efforts in which he is not yet completely engaged, serve him as experience for greater efficiency, and never fully compromise him. His forces are still intact. His ideals have become more defined by contact with reality, his experiences and his attempts have shown him his possibilities and traced for him the way of success. He is ready now to commit himself totally, with all his accumulated wealth, with his whole unified being, in an undertaking of salvation that will be his work, the work of his life and the fulfilment of his apostolic plans. Now he is capable of undertaking and of commanding; he is a man and a leader. The apostle is formed.

3. *The adult.*

It would seem that henceforward a sort of equilibrium is established in life. In one sense, that is true, the soul does avoid the fluctuations of feeling, the changes of direction of an adolescence that has not yet fixed its path. Charity takes on form in an action that assures its stability. The love of God is nourished by the very difficulty of what one undertakes for Him. It seems then that the spiritual life advances in the very tempo of the development of the apostolic influence, and that it blossoms out while giving off its light. There would be progress, but in continuity, ascent but along the same lines. However, in the depths of the soul, at the very center where his apostolic vocation is formed, a new crisis is being delineated.

Now his progress will no longer take place in a continuous line, but according to a new interior movement and a sort of unexpected overturning of his perspectives of action. Because this crisis is generally unfolded more slowly than the crisis of adolescence and is often crystallized only after years of work, it is less noticed. Because it no longer goes on beneath the vigilant look of attentive educators, but at times in a great spiritual solitude and under the regard of God alone, its evolution has perhaps been studied less. And yet, because it reaches souls generously dedicated in order to purify them, because it results either in a growth which is an ascension onto a new level of interior life and a transformation in the manner of efficacy of action, or in a falling back, a sort of discouragement which is fatal as well to prayer as to the apostolate; because, in order to co-operate with grace, it is extremely useful to grasp spiritually the interior meaning of one's action, it is of the greatest importance to see, finally, in what this new phase of the apostolic life consists, and where that road begins which leads to new perspectives.

At the starting point of this crisis there is a discovery —an astonishing and painful discovery—the same one of which Péguy speaks in those unforgettable pages of *Clio* which he consecrates to the man of forty. "See," he says, "it is History that speaks, this man of forty. Perhaps we know this Péguy, our man of forty. Perhaps we are beginning to hear of him. He is forty, he therefore knows. The knowledge that no teaching can give, the secret that no method can prematurely confide . . . the instruction that no school can impart, he has . . . First of all, he knows who he is . . . But above all, he knows that he knows. For he knows the great secret of every creature, the secret that is the most universally known and yet has never filtered through; the secret that is the most universally divulged and which has never passed from the men of forty past thirty-seven, past thirty-five, past thirty-three years, has never gone down to the men below. He knows that people are not happy." [4]

Let us not hear in these words the echo of an absolute pessimism. We know well enough that Péguy is the lyricist of hope, we do not take him for one disenchanted with life. It is rather the affirmation of a law of human growth, and the entrance to that narrow passageway which is the vestibule of the mystery of the second virtue.

Psychologists who study the depths of the soul have seen it. On their chart of the evolution of affectivity, they have indicated for all not only the crisis of adolescence, but the even more profound transformation of mature age. Here is man, at the middle of his life. Up to now all the forces of his soul have been tending ahead toward a plan to be carried out. This tension sustains his effort and maintains the dynamic equilibrium of his psychic life. The effort of thought and action in order to secure a position, to develop his business, to acquire a reputation, or a fortune. The impetus of the heart, in order to find a mate, to found a home, to develop his family, to raise his children.

Now his position is established; brilliant or mediocre, it has been obtained. He can see nothing more than the modification of details that do not change the essential

---

[4] Chas. Péguy, *Clio*, Paris, Gallinard, pp. 175-176.

content of his life. Already now its traits are fixed and its ultimate success or nonsuccess mark them forever. People know, as in the case of a dead man, what he has been. His family has reached its full development in accordance with its human possibilities, and circumstances. His children are growing up with their riches and their limitations, and that cannot be changed either. They too, in their way, by their very presence, put their parents back into the preceding generation . . . into the past.

Thus come to his midpoint, he must now perceive all of life suddenly turning upside down, and before him the downgrade that leads to death. From the eminence of this instant which dominates the past and the future, his eyes measures what his life has been. And indeed, it is necessary to note that whereas it has been all of those things, that is all it has been—irremediably so.[5] Therefore, at times the disproportion between the plans of adolescence, those long-cherished, ardently-pursued dreams, and this reality whose outlines are finally fixed, bursts forth. And, as human forces lack the power to change that, to make things over, there is nothing henceforward to polarize the forces of life, there is no more future, no project ahead to sustain the tension of effort.

The soul can no longer look its destiny in the face. It hides this fundamental disillusion from itself by distractions that cannot satisfy it. That is the risk . . . if this falling behind of human enterprises and the ebb of time do not lead to an abandonment of the spiritual life.

It is impossible to number and describe all the forms

---

[5] Cf. Chas. Péguy, *Victor-Marie, Comte Hugo,* in *Cahiers de la Quinzaine,* Oct. 23, 1910. "Forty is an implacable age. It does not allow itself to be deceived any more. It tells us no more stories . . . it hides nothing . . . Everything is unveiled, everything is revealed. Everything is betrayed . . . For it is the age when we become what we are."

this painful, central, intuition may take. There are as many as there are individuals. There is the spinster of forty who now knows that she will not marry and that forever, there will be lacking to her the support and the affection of a spouse, the crown of children of whom she still dreams. There is the young widow of forty, who knows that her life is ultimately frustrated and humanly broken by a separation which has taken from her a support, a tenderness, that she needed. There is the household which knows that it will not have any children, and that an immense tenderness, made to give itself, will remain forever unused. There is the sick man who, after the final relapse that leaves no further hope, knows that he will never be able to get married, or work like everybody else, or finally, to fulfill those dreams he has borne within him for so many years and toward which he has bent so many efforts and faltering steps. The bitter knowledge of the failure of dreams is the secret of so many hearts. Each one bears its own wound. These are things we cannot tell. And we have to reflect a long time before telling them to ourselves, for who knows whether he will be able to bear the terrible news?

This, which is true for so many others, will again hold true, in a new and so to speak, aggravated manner, for the apostolic life. This crisis, the man engaged in action will experience, especially as an apostle.

It is here in fact that the painful disproportion between the faintly perceived ideal and the fulfilments already achieved especially appears. Sometimes this revelation comes all of a sudden, as an excruciating shock; more often it comes about slowly, by the action of a whole series of experiences, which vary with each person as does life itself, and result in the same trial for all.

First of all, in a trial of personal life. Often, in the drive of initial generosity, and of a more sensible grace which lights and buoys up the beginnings of the spiritual life, sanctity seems near and almost easy. Difficulties are indeed envisaged, but they are represented rather than lived. Moral reforms are resolute, but they are foreseen rather than carried out. The atmosphere itself of the environment of formation, and a psychology of youth which leads to enthusiasm, render the illusion easier.

It is necessary to discover oneself slowly; to learn to measure the tenacity of interior oppositions, the subtlety and the snares of sin. Here are resolutions a hundred times made and a hundred times to be remade. Sin is no longer just something like a stain that we clean up, but alas, an impregnation so deep-seated that it seems to become one flesh with us, and to be able to disappear only with death. We may change environments, frames of reference and occupations, our sin is there, against us. It rediscovers itself, transforms itself, adapts itself. We may have dreamed of one day offering a perfect life, but here we can only give a sinner who each day measures more and more, how much he needs to be saved.

Nevertheless, the adult is so strongly involved in his action that if the success of his apostolate were perfect, this failure of personal success would be easily masked. But most often it is in the domain of action that the bitterest disillusions await us. If we compare ourselves, not to an apostolic ideal already amputated by life and narrowed by experience, but to our initial ambition of shining forth, of conversion, of the transformation of souls, environments and institutions, what a waste! Action has forced us to cut back! Which one of us has not caught the saddened mien of the mature man when he hears young people discuss reforms to be undertaken, works to be created? We too had thought we would do great things . . . and here we have been at work for years now, and have fallen far short.

Now we have had the experience of the resistance of the environment. We do not know that when we have not acted. We make plans and believe that it is enough to will it in order for them to be carried out. We imagine reforms and think that it is enough to speak for them to enter into morality. We confound thought with reality, the plan with the edifice. Between the two there is a world to move, to raise up, to organize. It is heavy; sometimes it is crushing. It fights back.

To this resistance which comes from man is often added that which comes from things. We run up against economic conditions, physical miseries, political events, which are not dependent on us and on which hangs the success of our apostolate. We feel ourselves seized, constrained, crushed, by an enormous and complex world of material conditionings, too heavy for us to be able to raise up.

Finally, it is perhaps the helps we could most legitimately count on, the support of friends and of leaders, that come to fail. We have not found the human understanding and the supernatural relationships we were hoping for. Where we were expecting a support, we find an obstacle. Our misunderstood plans stagnate and end up rotting with an odor of death. Thus, the man who had started out with such a fine impetus sometimes finds himself, after several years, disconcerted by events, deceived by other people, disillusioned with himself, strangely poor and alone. What are we to say if on top of this abandonment by men, there rests the silence of

God? For at times it is true that Jesus Himself seems
absent; we have to walk in this darkness, persevere in this
void . . . but where are we to go?

Is it then necessary, someone may say, to set up, at
the very heart of the apostolate a law of pessimism and a
necessity for failure? No, of course, and we think that,
on the contrary, an action well-thought out and cou-
rageously undertaken, must give some good results. If it
were otherwise, we would have to question ourselves
seriously. But if we have to formulate a law, it is that the
more the apostle's life unfolds, the more accomplishments appear in their precise—and whatever their success, always limited—outlines, whereas the desire to save
becomes more and more swift and unlimited. Henceforth, a painful, gradually increasing contrast appears between the initial plan, the intention of an entire life, the
germ of desire, the love which extends to all, and the
action, the fulfilment, the life which has done so little
good and for so few people. If there has to be a law, this
is the law: that what man accomplishes is not in propor-
tion to what he desires. We do not do what we should
like to have done. The heart of an apostle is always
larger than his action, and a dying Vincent de Paul can
feel that he has done nothing.

4. *The old man.*

What to say if we pursue experience unto old age. Let
us speak of a beautiful old age, the kind which crowns a
well-filled life. Activities drop off, one after the other; it
is necessary to reduce one's sphere of action, to resign
one's functions, to be replaced by younger people . . . to
see one's ideas, one's methods, set aside for new formulas.

Does a man have to give up being an apostle? To feel himself progressively diminished and useless? Humanly, it would seem so.

But perhaps that is only a human view of things, and perhaps, on the contrary, it is necessary for us to discover a center of supernatural perspective wherein the life of the apostle, through the deployment of his action, raises itself progressively toward a new mode of communicating the divine blessings. His radiance, far from reaching an apogee only to tend thereafter to decline, would be but a dawn whose light would grow impalpably greater throughout all of life, until the day of eternity. A new viewpoint this, which would permit us to go around the impasse in which we have seen action become entangled, and to come victoriously forth from this spiritual crisis of the adult period, not by consenting to diminution, but by accepting a purification.

II. SPIRITUAL PROGRESS

We have tried to sketch the psychological attitudes which are normally found in the adolescent, the young man, the adult and the old man, in the face of action. One would be tempted to discover a sort of psychological rhythm which takes possession of our interior evolution and draws us on in spite of ourselves. There is no such thing. Whereas a certain evolution of mentality is imposed on the totality of men, by virtue of this same evolution, the soul is invited to make choices that are more and more profound and perfectly free. The spiritual life remains a great drama in which, amid the unfolding of psychological laws, grace and freedom unceasingly act.

This evolution is a trial. It is possible that this psy-

chological maturing of the life of action, and especially
of the apostolic life, give rise to spiritual progress. It is
also possible that the soul, falling short of the effort demanded of it, not daring to commit itself on the level
which is proposed to it, shirks the final stages and the
ultimate purifications. It may thereby miss its full spiritual evolution and the fulness of its apostolic effulgence.
Saint John of the Cross outlined it in the frontispiece of
the *Ascent of Carmel*: there are easy roads which wind
around at medium elevation on the flank of the mountain, but which do not reach the abrupt and barren
slopes that alone lead to the summit of contemplation.
It is thus with apostolic progress. On this side of the
mountain, too, the path that leads to the fulness of life
and of radiance is narrow.

1. *Poor reactions.*

What then are the easiest paths by which a person
may escape the rigors of a purely supernatural climate?
Faced with the trials that life causes the dreams of youth
to undergo, the adult may react in different ways.

Some, to begin with, avoid the crisis we have described. They resolve this contrast between the ideal perceived and the fulfilment obtained at the expense of the
ideal. They stoically heal that painful tension between
the desires of the soul and its capabilities by reducing the
desire to the dimensions of reality. In a word, they resign
themselves. They treat as reveries the projects of youth.
They have lost their illusions. They amuse themselves
over those of younger people. No dream is ever realized—
that will never happen. They have understood their
limitations. Perhaps at first they resented them deeply,

but now they have accepted them, they resolutely en-
trench themselves in them, they make a law of life out
of them. They accept no further novelty, they are no
longer seeking to go beyond.

2. *The resigned.*

For the pessimists or those whom life has misused,
this resignation will be accomplished with sadness—these
are bitter resigners. We too had dreamed, we had hoped
to transform the world, but now, the best part of life has
passed and our action is going into a decline, and nothing
shows as yet. Disenchanted apostles who continue to
work with conscientiousness, but whose action is not
shot through with a living faith in success. A sort of resentment drives them to darken and destroy all the enthusiasm of youth. All initiative finds them skeptical.
They expect, as a personal victory, the failure of inno-
vators. How discouraging they are to those who work
with them! Lives henceforward without drive, which at
times try to conceal their emptiness from themselves in
more or less noble diversions ranging from profane studies to odd jobs, and are so many parasites on apostolic
labor.

For others, more optimistic, or for whom life may
have set aside some applauded results or some personal
preferment, this resignation will be made in the aura of
success. These are the satisfied ones—satisfied with what
they have done and with what they have been. A certain
widening perspective, a particular outlook in which the
results obtained conceal the immensity of what ought
to have been done, a certain inflation of their activities,
permits them to think without too much anxiety about

the world and about themselves. These too, in their own way, have sacrificed the ideal to reality. And because it is terribly laborious to make others—to make ourselves—believe that we have succeeded, they believe they are working. Alas! They have sacrificed reality itself. But in order to close up this distance that separates it from desire, they prefer to live in illusion.

3. *The despairing.*

Others, finally, and these among the best, turn from easy solutions; they do not resign themselves. Their immense apostolic desire is too profoundly rooted in their souls for them to be able to renounce it without denying themselves. They have not consented to cutting back any part of the drives of their youth. It is always the same desire to save without limits that animates them. They too have had to note the limits of their action, the resistance of the environment, the failure of expected helps, the deficiencies of their personal forces, but they have not accepted defeat. The tension between the intention, largely catholic, and the realizations, so narrowly limited, remains intact and vibrant. Then it is they suffer. They suffer terribly. They ask themselves strange questions: is it necessary to renounce the ideal of perfection, as others have done? The vast plans formerly so dearly nurtured? Is it necessary to say: it was a dream of youth, a folly? Or, in order to fulfill them at last, to escape the impossible way of an action which has no ending, is it necessary to flee to the Trappists? Life seems to be all the more painful a failure, the less the soul seeks to veil from itself this flagrant disproportion between reality and the ideal.

Therefore, around it circulates the temptation of resentment; resentment against superiors who did not know how to utilize its possibilities, resentment against the flock that has not listened and toward which one becomes severe and at times harsh, resentment against oneself, against life, against the Church, against God Himself Who does not grant prayer and does not respond to what one expected of Him. A deadly atmosphere for the interior life, which lacks peace and confidence. A dangerous atmosphere for action, which risks lacking drive, initiative, joy, because it tends despairingly toward a goal it knows it will never reach.

What is to be done then to get out of this crisis? If it is necessary neither to turn against the initial impetus to content ourselves with reality, nor inflate the reality of the results in order to see in them the realization of the ideal, nor yet to live painfully and despairingly in this irreducible tension between plan and reality? Are we not at an impasse?

Here there is no more path. To go on it is necessary to climb, in an abrupt way, onto a new level. It is necessary to accept a new method of conceiving one's action. It is necessary to consent to being purified.

4. The good reaction: being purified.

What does it mean to be purified? First we must consent to the light. We must recognize that we need to be purified. The work of the Holy Spirit in a soul which consents to His action, consists first of all in convincing it of its sin. We must agree to see that; whereas these apostolic desires which lead us to action come from God, they also come from ourselves and carry along in their agitated stream both the best that is in us and the less good. This powerful stream is as yet impure. As St. Gregory accurately remarks in his *Pastoral:* "Very often, indeed, the soul lies to itself in what concerns it. It imagines that it seeks no part of the world's glory in its good works, whereas it still loves that." [6] Thus it is with our best projects: the love of God, the love of others and self-love are strangely mingled in them. Following a pattern which is habitual where we are concerned, we are inclined to call the mixture by the name of the noblest ingredient—desire of apostolate.

Now, the light of God reveals to us these traces of self-love in action. This impassioned desire to succeed, to do well, to do better than the others, does not have as its only wellspring the concern for saving, but also that of arousing admiration. We recognize this in the exaggerated need for making known the good accomplished, for showing it off, especially before our leaders. That spite regarding a failure, this severity toward the defection or error of a fellow team-worker, does not have as its only reason anxiety for souls, but the fear of personal failure. How difficult it is, when someone gives himself to a work, whether it be a movement, a house of education, a pious group or a parish, not to promote himself secretly while promoting the work. Personal ambition, the desire to be a leader, the looked-up-to moving force, is confounded with the just concern for the group one is directing, and hides itself from its own eyes behind this social alibi.[7]

---

[6] St. Gregory, *Le Pastoral*, Ed. de Maredsous, p. 25.

[7] cf. Boulard, *Essor ou declin du clergé français*, p. 283. Among the qualities demanded of the priest by laymen: "disinterestedness: at times we feel ourselves used by him, instead of his helping us to fulfill our mission".

Nevertheless, this leaven of self-love in the inmost intentions threatens to falsify our relationships with God, as well as our relationships with men. If we no longer have a simple outlook, the unique intention of pleasing God, the whole organism of our activities is upset. A human project of personal advancement blocks from our eyes great supernatural perspectives and prevents our concentrating the interior regard on the infinite that is the pure will of God. The soul wastes its time in vain pursuit of vain success, it is no longer in the loving and confident attitude of the child which seeks only to please its Father: it is no longer simple. It is playing on two levels and loses both ways.

A too-personal outlook is like a screen between us and God . . . we will be able to find Him fully only when we shall have left it completely behind. But it is just as much of a screen between us and other people. Every apostle who is monopolized by a personal project that has to be carried out becomes incapable of opening himself truly to *the other fellow* and to receive him. He is not available . . . he is always distracted. If he listens to someone else it is in order to introduce him into his designs; if he bothers with him, it is in order to make him go along with his plan; if he directs him, it is in part to monopolize him.

It would be impossible to mention all the practical deviations which such attitudes entail. In order to inflate statistics, to obtain a flourishing result, we cannot accept the slow action of grace and of men's responses. We risk not respecting enough the liberty of souls, the proper orientation of their vocation. We push, we compel, at times we do violence, in order to obtain the realization of our project—which arouses reactions, retreats, divisions, struggles. Sometimes, on the other hand, we flatter, we pretend, we enter upon a kind of politics which seeks the approbation of all at the price of a lessening of the truth and the loss of savor of the Gospel.

How often is it that these aims of secret ambitions provoke among apostolic workers, among movements, even among religious congregations, jealousies, criticisms, that wound souls and ruin works. All of that proceeds from the same source: an intention that is insufficiently purified.

5. *The action of God, purification of imperfections.*

That is why God goes to work. Like a meticulous vinekeeper, He bends over His vine. It is to the apostolic worker that the words of St. John well apply: "Every branch that bears fruit, the Father will cleanse that it may bear more fruit." [8] The branches of our vain desires fall, one after the other. They seemed full of sap, but they were only parasites. The action of Providence cuts them off ruthlessly. How well it knows just where it is necessary to strike! It seems to devastate; in reality it purifies for a more abundant harvest.

But this action of God which makes use of the very circumstances of life and of the intervention of men, puts us up against a new choice. It is no longer, as in the days of our youth, a matter of choosing the good and of engaging in action—it is necessary to consent to a tearing away. Here the narrow way opens that permits us to go beyond outlooks on apostolic action that are too natural, that were leading to an impasse. We must purify our

---

[8] John, 15, 2-3.

action. We have to see that everything that falls is our personal plans, our ambitions, our egotism. But what remains, and more lively than ever, is adherence to the will of God for us, with the certitude that it is a will for salvation. In a word, we have to renounce our dreams, in order to keep the ideal intact. We have to leave behind every personal plan, in order to give ourselves entirely to the plan of God. Only a total confidence, animated by a purer love, can permit this surpassing of all our interests, so long and so avidly pursued. Here can be adapted to the apostolic laborer what St. John of the Cross writes of the contemplative: "In the secret still-room I drank of my Beloved: upon coming out, I knew nothing any more of the plain; I lost the flock that I was still following . . ." [9]

This purification of the intention presupposes a new and more supernatural way of looking upon the efficacy of action. At the moment we speak this total "yes" to the Will of the Father which strips us of so many plans, we have to consider that this divine Will can bring to fruition our desire of salvation in a way that goes beyond us. Thus, in agreeing to see our manner of saving sometimes fail, we are not breaking up the root of our desire of salvation, but are inserting it into the design of God. Here we were being a bit Jewish still and had, each of us, brought along our plan of triumphant Messianism. We have to see it broken, and like the Apostles, discover the plan of God, accept the mystery of the Cross. In this light everything is illuminated, and we finally realize that the Redemption of the world is not

---

[9] St. John of the Cross, *Canticle spirituel*, trans. by Dom Chevalier, p. 38, Desclee de Brouwer.

effected primarily by our success, but by our passion united to that of Christ.

6. *God purifies goodness.*

In the meantime, we must admit, the suppression of egotistical viewpoints and of personal ambitions in action is not enough to account for the conduct of God. We have to go further and deeper still. It is not only the lead and the rust that will be put into the crucible, but the gold itself, in order to be seven times purified. It is not only our dreams and our personal plans that are going to be put into question, but indeed the basic drive, the original desire, the very will to save . . . and not only the imperfect desires, but the good ones and even the best ones.

Indeed it is not a child of sin that God demands of Abraham, but the very son of the Promise. And that is but the image and the anticipation of that which goes on in Christ and in His Church. The Passion is the apparent failure not just of a man's plan, but of the plan of God Himself. It is the death of the Messias.

The Virgin at the foot of the Cross, daughter of Abraham, offers her Son to this design of God, which in some sort annihilates in Him His promises. But, like Abraham, she *believes* God to be powerful enough to continue His plan past failure and by this very failure itself; and to raise up life beyond death—and in this very trial itself.[10] Thus it is with the Church and the

---

[10] J. Danielou, *Mysterium futuri*, p. 104; Heb. 2, 17-19. "In faith Abraham offered Isaac . . . who had received the promises: thinking that God is capable of raising even from the dead: wherefore he accepted it also as a parable."

apostle. Every man who undergoes the action of God to the end is called upon to renew the sacrifice of Abraham, and to unite himself with the co-redeeming Virgin at the foot of the Cross. He has to sacrifice not only what is evil in himself . . . but what is best, that which he has conceived of God, which he has formed according to grace, that which he has done not for himself, but for God, even that which God has promised him and for which he has sacrificed everything. He still has to submit it and sacrifice it. Why these demands by God? So that it might be quite clear and affirmed anew, that what is loved is not the gifts of God, but God Himself Who gives them, and that what makes for our assurance is not success already obtained, but pure confidence in the power of God.

Through the fall of all his desires, and after the apparent failure of all the designs of God, and the ruin of his work, the apostle still has confidence. He is assured that ultimately, the last word will belong to Divine Faithfulness. The promise will be fulfilled. The root of his desire will bear its fruits. After the winter will come a marvelous flowering and, beyond death, God will raise up a new life. It is this imperturbable confidence in the fidelity of God that *obtains*, in the end, the superabundant accomplishment of his designs. And that is why it is this confidence, finally, that God works on, that He purifies, that He deepens, in order to have the joy of fulfilling it. For after all, we have to recognize that the last word of human activity is to evoke the action of God by the intensity of its hope. Therefore, in a total abnegation, the apostle finds his ultimate blossoming and his perfect mode of action, for the immensity of what he obtains corresponds to the catholicity of his initial desire.

III. PRACTICAL CONSEQUENCES

1. *Light on the apostolic life.*

We must recognize that all the imperfect attitudes we have described proceed radically from the same refusal to enter into this purely supernatural view of the value of action, as an appeal to the intervention of God, and from the same recoiling before the Mystery. Whether we are satisfied with our apparent results or despair because of their mediocrity, we retain a purely natural way of considering action and the manner of its efficacy. We are afraid to go beyond this human point of view. Is that not due to a sort of latent rationalism which drives us to refuse that which goes beyond us, and to hold us to what is in our size, by rejecting the smallness and the superhuman splendors of the plan of God? We are afraid to believe because we are afraid to have confidence, we are afraid of seeming naive. Only the little ones and the humble may enter here.

But if consent is not given to all that is disconcerting and superhuman in the Divine plan of salvation, we sink into darkness. We no longer understand the conduct of God. We are no longer going in the direction of God. Difficulties and failures seem to be the sign of an abandonment by the Providence of the Father, when they are, on the contrary, multiplied indications by which He urges us to ascend closer to Him . . . a formidable lack of comprehension of God's views which adds an even more cruel suffering to the sufferings of life, that of no longer having any grasp of its meaning.

Quite to the contrary, if we do consent, everything becomes illuminated. It is even while giving consent to

these abnegations that we grasp their meaning, and that
we discover the intent of this purifying intervention of
God. In all these tribulations, the soul grasps in a supernatural light the action of God within it. Through it, it
is stripped of all its personal ambitions, it knows that it
is in order to have access to a greater love and to a
greater radiating forth through a more total confidence.

And just as the mystic finds in this very darkness and
this sort of absence by which God detaches him from
every imperfect thought, a new and mysterious Presence,
so too in these very abandonments, the man of action
discovers the vigilant protection of the Father, and
grasps more strongly the hand that God tends to him.
He leans less on himself and more on God. He is growing in hope.

This is in fact the ultimate meaning of such apostolic
purification: it is a purification of hope. While growing,
theological Hope sets off more and more purely what
the theologians call its formal motive. That is, we lean
less and less on our own plans, on our own resources, or
even on results already achieved, on our merits and efforts, on graces already received . . . but uniquely and
simply, as says St. Thomas, on the all-powerfulness and
the infinite mercy of the Father of Heaven.[11] That is
why the feeling of our poverty and of our impotence does
not prevent in any way the greatest apostolic ambitions.
It is in our littleness that God accomplishes great things.
It is our poverty that He is pleased to fill up, and it is
empty nets that He fills with the miraculous catch.

This confidence will be apostolic. It will not be a

---

[11] *Sum. theol.* II[a] II[ae], q. 18, a. 4, ad 2[m]. "Hope does not shine
forth principally on grace already obtained, but on the divine omnipo-
tence and mercy . . ."

waiting for personal salvation, of a triumph over self—but an apostle's hope, and an expectation which indissolubly concerns the pastor and his flock. Is it possible to hope thus for others? In this too, St. Thomas, with the tranquil boldness which is customary in him, gives us the formula for this apostolic hope. "If one presupposes," says he, "an union of love with other men, then we may desire and hope for a good for them as for ourselves." [12] How true that is with regard to the apostolic worker and those for whom he has given his heart and his life. Truly, before God, he forms but one now with them, and that is why he hopes from God for himself and for them. There is but one hope and it is apostolic. Finally, it is the awaiting of the day of Christ and of His triumphant, salvific return.

This hope is efficacious. It obtains from God that which it expects from Him. More, God puts it into the heart of man in order to have the joy of fulfilling it. And man experiences his confidence during the night only because he already sees the day during which it will be rewarded. The desire of the saints could hardly be vain.[13] This desire for the salvation of mankind that grace causes to rise in their heart is already the sign that we are in a saved world.

That is why the apostle is not astonished at so many difficulties, oppositions, persecutions, which provoke him to a purer confidence in God alone. He knows that this is the summit of his apostolic action. All these failures do not discourage him, for now he sees that through

---

[12] *Sum. theol.* II^a II^{ae}, q. 17, a. 3. "Praesupposita unione amoris ad alterum, jam aliquis potest desiderare et sperare aliquid alteri sicut sibi."

[13] cf. *Sum. theol.* III^a, q. 78, a. 1. "The perfect desire of the saints cannot be vain."

them the divine plan of salvation is accomplished. Each branch of his human desires that falls is so much sap that rises in the Tree of the Redemption. Therefore, these trials seem transformed. No longer are they the limitations against which the realization of our fondest desires stumbles; they are the means of fulfilling our ideal, the instrument of this work desired among all others—the salvation of men. They will all and always be for us the cross on which the apostle meets Jesus Christ in the act of His priesthood and with Him saves the world.

Therefore, the crisis which we have described is finally unknotted without having to sacrifice either reality or the ideal. The adult will be a realist and will be able to see things as they are, in the bareness of their poverty, but keeps intact his desire to save and remains an enthusiast, because, more than ever, he believes in final victory and in the salvation of the world.

It is also on the supernatural plane, and only in this pure light that comes from the Cross, that we are able to solve so many painful situations—of which we have spoken, and to discover the meaning not only of all apostolic action, but doubtless also, of all human life . . . and certainly of all human death.

Wasted lives in which the need to love has not succeeded in being satisfied, in which the desire to give oneself has not been able to flourish, in which the bonds of affection have been prematurely snapped, in which the plan of action has been stopped by circumstances or by physical failing . . . in which, in a thousand and one ways, the basic desire of the soul, that which seems to be its first calling, appears to have failed. What are we to think of them? Are they the refuse of a world too hard, or were they put there to allow others to flourish? Not at all. They are the sorrowful and bleeding witnesses of the law of the Cross. For them, the all-important thing is to discover Its meaning. Christ must make them enter into His paschal mystery and after that, teach them that this state of complete stripping in which they seem to be displayed before the world and suspended by the very tearing out of their wounds, is a narrow path which leads to life. . . . By this very stripping away, if it is offered up with confidence, *every bit* of affection and love, of desire for fecundity and for giving which they bear in themselves, will find its fruition beyond all expectations. Strange vocations, terrible vocations. It is for them that it is written: *he who loses his life saves it.*

But no, that is written for everyone. For years and days come for every man when his forces decline, in which his bereavement unties one by one all the bonds of his earthly affections, when weakness stops one by one all his earthly activities, when he falls, exhausted, finished. Is that a decline? Humanly, it is death. Christianly, it is the Cross. And at that very hour when everything, perhaps, that he has tried to build is crumbling, if he consents to the plan of God, if he affirms his unfailing confidence in His fidelity, then he enters into those new bonds of grace with those whom he loves, then he effects the salvation of those for whom he is immolated, then he sees his dearest hopes accomplished in a disconcerting but infinitely more beautiful way than anything he had dreamed of. At this hour when he leaves the earth and the rough outlines of his abandoned projects that he has left there, he enters into the eternal, and slowly discovers the grand plan of God in which all his desires are satisfied. His final failure is his most brilliant success, and this ultimate suffering the richest of all his actions, the one which compensates for the weakness of all the others, and this death finally, a source of life, and this night, the dawn of a new day.

2. *Light on apostolic action.*

Still, we might fear lest such a purification of the natural desire to act, such a remitting of one's whole being to God's design, result in a falling back of apostolic activity, a retreat before the initiatives to be taken, a fatalism which too easily sides with failures by seeing in them the action of God, and finally, in a sort of pious apathy.

There is none of that. It would be as false to confound the laziness of the man who does not want to undertake anything with the abandonment to Providence of the purified soul, as it would be to identify the natural sleep of the man who lets himself go to sleep during prayer with the prayer of quiet. In both cases there is a certain giving up of the natural manner of acting, but on behalf of a transformation onto a new level. In both cases there is danger of confusion, in a lazy resignation which falls below natural activity, and a supernatural resignation which rises above it. The loyal man makes no mistake about that.

The rule of an authentic purification is that it does not lie in the direction of the tendencies of a lazy nature in order to satisfy them, but grafts itself onto a vigorous activity and onto an action which is already generously dedicated, in order to purify them. It does not favor the happy-go-lucky approach, it impedes it, restricts it, in order to make it arise a powerful vital force: the Cross.

That is why, far from demanding a disenchanted skepticism before action, the apostolic life claims a total commitment. Far from preaching distrust for apostolic activity, it requires one to ask for courage to give oneself thereto. But this action is, itself, a path which rises and leads to perfection. This action normally is transformed. And if we consent to give ourselves to its natural rhythm, it leads us to disengage more and more our sense of submission to God, our sense of abandonment to His influence, of suffering in His hands.

Is there, then, a sort of contradiction at the heart of apostolic action, since, on the one hand, it always has to seek, by all human means, the success of its evangelizing enterprise, and on the other, it knows that this will never happen, and that it is through its very impotence that the power of God will be manifested? No, no contradiction, but mystery—it is the mystery of grace itself.

The action of God does not destroy the action of man, but accomplishes it by going beyond it. We must inscribe in the world the outline of our desires and the sketch of our plans . . . but they depend on God for their accomplishment. The ultimate effort of every human enterprise, when it has indicated by its work where its impetus is leading it, is to open itself to the intervention of God. Nature opens itself to grace, action is achieved in passion. Man gives himself completely back to his Creator. He seems to lose everything and he has gained everything. No, his action is not indifferent to the final result. . . . Everything comes from him, and everything comes from God. Everything comes from him as delivered to God. Everything comes from him as a preparation, everything comes from God as consummation. Everything proceeds from him as empty and as an invitation, and everything proceeds from God as fulness and as a response. But it is this very emptiness, consented to and held forth, which calls down the gift of God. And that is why all the labor of God in the apostolic man is not to suppress his work, but to make him feel more and more the catholic aspirations thereof, and, at the same time, its radical insufficiency, in order that it might finally result in a total giving of self which prepares its triumphant fulfilment.[14] The love of humanity becomes an intolerable suffering for the heart which does not transform it into Christian hope. It can only be in this pure supernatural light and in consent to this great mystery of demand and free giving that the apostle finds his balance.

Therefore, he continues to tend toward the goal to be achieved, toward the apostolic success to be obtained, for he knows that God wants this manifestation in the world of His redemptive love, and that it concurs with the work of salvation. But he does not despair at not arriving there right away, because he knows that his action is offered to the action of God in order to receive therefrom its fulfilment. Also, he acts with force, but in peace. He remains a realist and is able to see the deficiencies of his results, but he has through it all a confidence in the ultimate success, a joy, a security whose

---

[14] Caussade has well described this efficacy of the soul given over to the action of Providence: "It knows only how to abandon itself and to give itself into the hands of God to serve Him in the way He knows. Often it does not know what purpose it is serving, but God knows very well. Men think it useless . . . Yet it is still true that by secret resources and unknown channels it spreads abroad an infinity of graces on persons who often do not think of it and of whom it does not think. Everything is efficacious, everything preaches, everything is apostolic in these abandoned souls." *L'abandon à la Providence Divine,* I, p. 56.

contagion makes him capable of the greatest undertakings. Knowing his weakness, he fears nothing, because
he is leaning on God. His action moves in a climate of
offering, of confidence and of abandon which transform
it into habitual intimacy with God. His detachment
from immediate success permits him to be no longer so
much occupied in making others enter into his plans as
in loving them all with the very love of the Father Who
makes His sun shine down on the just and the unjust.
And this pure Charity is the most pressing of all invita-
tions. He is not an optimist, because now he knows what
there is in man and in himself, and that we are capable
of very little, but he is not a pessimist, because he knows
that God is capable of all and is infinitely good. He carries in himself the presentiment of those marvels which
God holds in reserve for those whom He loves, and he
knows that by the very weakness of our action, the
humiliation of our sufferings and the veritable ruin of
death, God is preparing to fulfill the immensity of our
desires.

In a word, he has gone beyond human attitudes . . .
that of the satisfied man who thinks to obtain results
by his own forces, that of the embittered man who de-
spairs of achieving success because his forces are insufficient; he has entered into the only attitude for a truly
filial soul, which is that of Hope.

5

JESUS CHRIST IN HIS CHURCH

I. THE PROGRESS OF THE APOSTLES IN THE KNOWLEDGE OF CHRIST

FRIENDSHIP IS A marvelous thing. We do not know whence it comes, nor where it goes. Who can tell its distant origin? Who can mark that instant in which the presence of another ceases to be a burden and becomes a joy? Who can ever say just where it will lead us, to what discoveries, to what devotion, to what demands and to what unknown joys? He who fashions a friendship becomes involved in a new world.

We like to speak of the "life" of friendship. It is true —a long friendship develops and is transformed like a living thing. There is continuity and progress. From childhood to maturity friendship expands. It resists changes of occupation and of mentality. It grows and is transformed through everything. Like a living thing, it possesses a force of assimilation; like a living thing, it has its rhythm. Events nourish it. Tribulations strengthen it. With the decline of years, we admire the way it has been enriched and deepened. We recognize its stages. The great events of life have indicated the phases of friendship. Each of these phases is a discovery and a transformation. We marvel at all the possibilities hidden in the initial seed. We recognize ourselves in fidelity to our friendships; we grow with their growth. We know, finally, that great friendships are the most beautiful fruit of the life of the spirit. "Blessed the man who has found a real friend." [1] For a long time we have believed that our friends are there to help us surmount the difficulties of life, but we are forced to say rather that all these events take place only to permit us to discover our friends.

All this is true of every human friendship. How much more is it of the friendship of Christ. God has willed to contract with us a friendship which takes root on the human plane in order to bear fruits of divine love. We must see that; in the light of God, it is the very meaning of our lives. The center of perspective according to which all events are ordered, is the development in ourselves of intimacy with Christ. The center of perspective according to which all human history is ordered is the marriage of humanity with Christ. At the end of all things there is this nuptial friendship according to which they finish by constituting but one—one only Mystical Christ given to the Father in the unity of the Spirit of Love. All events are mysteriously linked together for that purpose. We therefore have to discover, from an outlook based on wisdom, this secret harmony according to which everything in our lives concurs unto the knowl-

---

[1] *Ecclus.*, 25:12. (Translation based on French text.)

edge of and intimacy with, Christ. Without this, we no longer understand. In this light, everything is illuminated.

But this friendship between Christ and us has its rhythm, its phases and its crises. More exactly, all the rhythms of life, all the phases of life, all the crises of life, are ordered to the development and the deepening of the intimate knowledge of Christ. In truth, this friendship with Christ is our life. Our whole life is the growth of our true knowledge of Christ Jesus, in the participation of His mystery. Life, with its happenings, that which we see from the outside, with its interior unfolding, its fluctuations, its riches, its exigencies, its failures even, has no meaning, ultimately, except for the ripening of this secret fruit and for the sinking of this well of knowledge and of love which springs up unto eternity. He who has grasped this link between the unforeseen event, the concrete situation, the actual trial, and the knowledge of Christ, has understood the meaning of life; he is discovering its unity; he knows where he is going, he has found himself. This knowledge of Christ is the light which illumines the plan of God for him and for the world.

Nevertheless, as in everything that lives, there is here something disconcerting which throws off all calculations. How far will friendship go, how far will its demands reach? We cannot foresee that. That is why the man who commits himself to the bond of friendship always takes some kind of chance. How much more so, when this friendship binds us to God! The friendship of a very great man elevates us. It is exacting. Whether it be that of a genius of thought or that of a hero of action, it always expects from us a difficult and exalting transcendence of ourselves. It has some astonishing surprises in store for us. Still, in the very thing which upsets us and

goes beyond us, we feel that the best of our being is fulfilled; that is why we have been created. The friendship
of someone greater reveals us to ourselves.

But that remains just an image of the friendship of
Christ. Alone, this intimacy brings us to the most marvelous of surpassings, that of the divine life, in order to
make us discover what we are—sons of God. We must
not be astonished that its demands are total. The knowledge of Christ demands everything of us, in order to
transform everything in us.

Yet, we would like to know in what this total giving
which is required of us consists, this transformation
which must take place. We would like to know the
rhythm in which this life of friendship progresses. What
is it, then, truly to know Christ, and what discovery does
His intimacy bring us to? Has God told us nothing about
that which is most important for us, that which makes
our life? God reveals us these things not in theories, but
in facts. He does not describe His friendship; He makes
it live. It is enough to look at those who first lived in it
to know what it is, and at those who went all the way in
this friendship, to know how it proceeds.

Those who discovered, at the price of their total commitment, the knowledge of Christ, are the Apostles. They
are the first in this new phase of the intimacy of humanity with God, and they are models for all those who are
proceeding along this path. Their experience shows us
the way. The very rhythm and progress of their knowledge of Christ providentially light up our march toward
Him. Their whole life was discovering Christ. It must be
our whole life to follow them and to pass by the way
they went, in order to rejoin them where they are, with
Christ.

1. *From the banks of the Jordan to the crisis of Capharnaum.*

They first of all met this man who was called Jesus. It was an unforgettable day. The Synoptics and St. John have preserved for us the living memory of those days in which they were discovering Jesus. The whole Gospel can be understood as the account of the communication made to the world of their progress in the knowledge of the Lord.

Today we project upon this history the light of twenty centuries of reflection. Everything seems simple to us. Arrived at this summit, we discover in a single glance the whole outline of the road and the goal to which it leads. Thus we see in the Gospels the Son of God who reveals Himself progressively to these men. But at the time of the first discovery, they proceeded gropingly, beginning with the first contact with this man who John the Baptist had pointed out to them on the shores of the Jordan, toward a disconcerting knowledge of the Mystery of His divine origin.

At least, we would like to believe that they went from astonishment to astonishment, in an evergrowing light, toward this unheard-of discovery that they were in the presence of the very Word of God, which was addressed to them, and of the Word Incarnate. But in truth, we should rather say that they went from disappointment to disappointment, to the total darkness of Calvary, where they were obliged to recognize that they had as yet understood nothing and that in reality they did not know Him. More exactly, we have to say that the knowledge of Christ on the part of the Apostles developed according to the progression of the life of Christ itself, and proceeded according to the tempo of His paschal mystery. It was in participating in His mystery that the Apostles learned to know Him.

Not just once, but so to speak at each step, at least at each Pasch, a new crisis puts everything in doubt again. They have to see the ideas they had formed fall apart. They have the impression that what they had understood concerning Christ is escaping them. The light which they had glimpsed disappears. But this tribulation gives them access to a new level of knowledge of Christ. In this night itself, they see the dawning of a new light, which illumines His face with new radiance. It is a paschal night.

Doubtless the first miracles at Cana and Capharnaum made them discover in Jesus the mysterious Power of God. He is the envy of God, the expected Messias, He Who is to restore the Kingdom of Israel and return Worship to its splendor. "He manifested his glory and his disciples believed in Him." [2] However, "the Passover of the Jews was at hand and Jesus went up to Jerusalem." [3] Now He Who is to bring about the unity of the people comes into conflict with the leaders of the people. He Who is to restore Worship begins by chasing from the Temple the sheep and the bulls of the ritual sacrifices. These offerings have become the object of a commerce which horrifies Him. He Who is to give back to the Temple its former splendor announces its ruin. Is He then not the Messias people were waiting for? The religious leaders ask Him by what right He takes this revolutionary attitude. Who is He to act thus? Who am I? You will see on the day of My Passion. "Destroy this

---

[2] John 2:11.
[3] John 2:13.

temple, and in three days I will raise it up." [4] The Apostles do not understand these words; it is only a long time after, in the light of His Resurrection, that they will grasp their meaning. Yet a new light begins to dawn in their night: already a pale ray of paschal brightness. A dent is made in their conception of the Messias. Jesus is not the Messias as they were expecting Him. Might He not be the Messias as God is preparing Him: "They remembered that it is written: The zeal for thy house has eaten me up." [5]

One year later. The miracles have been renewed, which has multiplied the adherents. But the affirmations of independence with respect to the Jewish spirit have also multiplied, which has stiffened the opposition. A new crisis is in the making. A new Passover in Jerusalem. Jesus thinks of His Passion which is approaching. He announces the mystery of the Eucharist and that of His Cross, indissolubly linked in this paschal celebration. One year ahead of time, it is already the entire Passion. It is the paschal mystery which is in progress in the life of Jesus and in the heart of His Apostles—the mystery of Death and of Resurrection.

The discourse on the Bread of Life marks a sort of definitive rupture with popular enthusiasm. The spell of the miracles seems broken. Already there is failure and already the rejection of the Messias by His people, and not only by the people, but by His very disciples. "Many of his disciples therefore, when they heard this, said: This is a hard saying. Who can listen to it?" [6] The Apostles themselves are troubled and divided concerning Him.

---

[4] John 2:19.
[5] John 2:17.
[6] John 6:61.

Their faith is shaken and put into doubt. Jesus watches this dispersion of His followers before the exigencies of His mystery. "Jesus, knowing in himself that his disciples were murmuring at this, said to them: Does this scandalize you!" [7] The more He reveals Himself, the less the Jews are able to understand Him. This light blinds them. They reject what goes beyond them. They refuse Christ-according-to-God. "From this time many of his disciples turned back and no longer went about with him." [8] Concerning one of the twelve He has chosen, Jesus is obliged to say: "He is a devil." Already he has betrayed his Master and has killed Him in his heart.

Yet, at his very hour, a new knowledge of Christ begins for the small remainder of the faithful. This definitive break with the aims of the earthly ambitions of the crowd places Christ on His true plane. He is the Messias, as God gives Him. St. Peter proclaims it: "Thou art the Christ, the Son of the living God." [9] This knowledge of faith which the Father places in his soul is already Christ living in him no longer to die, He Whom flesh and blood are impotent to discover and Whom the Father alone engenders in those Whom He loves.

From that time forward, the Passion and the Resurrection of Christ are announced in souls. But it will be necessary to wait another year before the final passage of Christ to His Father is accomplished and before His glory appears unto His own. It is only in the light of these final events that the Apostles will understand all that has gone on before, it is only in the radiance of the Cross

---

[7] *John* 6:62.
[8] *John* 6:67.
[9] *Matt.*, 16:16. Cf. *John* 6:70.

that they will discover the Son of God and will know themselves before Him.

2. *The paschal mystery.*

The days of His Passion, of His death, of His burial and of His Resurrection, mark for the Apostles a final crisis in the knowledge of Christ. It is only beginning from that moment that they truly know Him.

That which nowadays strikes us the most in the Passion of Christ is the intensity of His sufferings, but what the Apostles saw in it at first was the failure of His mission; more precisely, the final ruin of all the ideas, all the earthly projects, all the plans which they had conceived regarding the mission of Christ. Up to the end of Christ's life, even more, up to the very day of Pentecost, the Apostles will maintain, along with the people, the idea of a triumph that would insure the political liberation of Israel and the restoration of the Kingdom of God. When Jesus, resurrected, promises the coming of the Spirit on the day of Pentecost, the Apostles still ask: "Lord, wilt thou at this time restore the kingdom to Israel?" [10] It is difficult for us to measure how profoundly this expectation is anchored in their religious mentality, even more difficult to measure to what extent this subverts their reactions. How many personal desires, human ambitions, earthly projects, are hidden behind this ideal of liberation! Disputes about precedence at the time of the Last Supper show very well the small extent to which minds are as yet opened to the true perspectives of the Kingdom of Heaven. How little they have understood the spiritual sense of the mission of Christ and the paradoxi-

---

[10] *Acts* 1:7.

cal manner in which He must take possession of His Kingdom—by humiliations and the Cross! Peter shows it again, when he wants to defend Jesus by the sword. That indeed is what it is all about!

To the end, then, they have understood nothing! Their attachment to Christ is sincere, their involvement in His following is real. Yes, they are always ready to die for Him. But always they picture Him as the Messias of whom they had dreamed. They see Him as liberator and triumphant. After three years of life in common, they still do not know Him. They do not know what kind of Messias and what kind of King He is in the plans of God. They do not know what triumph awaits Him beyond the Cross. They do not have the sense of God. They have not grasped the transcendence of the divine plan which surpasses all human projects and expectations.

The Passion is to be the final revelation of Christ to the Apostles. It is here that His divinity at last appears, His transcendence with respect to all human thoughts. It is at the same time, for the Apostles, the ultimate test of their faith in Christ. "Simon, Simon, behold, Satan has desired to have you, that he may sift you as wheat." [11] "You will all be scandalized this night; for it is written, I will smite the shepherd and the sheep will be scattered." [12] Crisis of their adherence to Christ, in the deepest sense: purification, pouring off. Every human expectation is ruined, every human forecast upset, every Jewish hope disappointed, all that they thought they had understood escapes them.

"We were hoping," [13] they will say, it is over. We

---

[11] *Luke* 22:31.
[12] *Mark* 14:27.
[13] *Luke* 24:21.

had hoped for the victory of the Jews over the Romans, under the leadership of the Messias. Supreme derision! The leaders of the people seized the Messias and obtained from the Romans permission to crucify Him. The people ratified their leadership: "Let him be crucified, let him be crucified!" Total and irremediable overthrow of every hope of liberation. It seems that faith in the Messias will fall with the same blow. How still to believe in the Messianism of Him Who is rejected by His people, in the triumph of the conquered one, in the liberation of the people by Him Who is in agony and is dead, in the design of God for Him Who appears to be abandoned by God? For that is the worst of it—that the envoy of God seems tragically rejected.

The faith of the Apostles is shaken. That of Judas has long since yielded. From the first rupture of Christ with political Messianism, Judas no longer follows Him with his heart in it. He has chosen his own plan of salvation in preference to that of God. He has chosen what is in his measure rather than leave himself open to the measure of God. He has chosen what is close to hand, what can be counted, felt, banked, rather than this future of mystery of which Christ gives a glimpse. And those thirty pieces of silver for which he delivers the Son of God are but the sign of a treason consummated long since in his heart, and the symbol of a more sordid greed, one by which he has preferred his human ideas about the Messias to the very plan of God.

The other Apostles now enter upon the supernatural plane, at the price of a painful stripping away. When the design of God begins to appear, it is blinding, it is upsetting. The Apostles no longer understand; they are in the dark. Now it is no longer a matter just of leaving

one's boat and one's nets. It is a whole mentality of
which one has to let himself be stripped. The purification attains the spirit. They have followed Christ, but,
in the way they represented Him to themselves, they saw
Him through a world of human ideas, of Jewish concep-
tions about the Messias. Now that He appears before
them irremediably stripped of these human sentiments,
they do not recognize Him.

They have not denied their love. Jesus remains their
Master. They will soon find themselves reunited in His
name. But how is their faith to accommodate itself to
what they have seen and to what has taken place? That
they do not understand. How can the Cross enter into
the plan of God? How can the Messias be crucified?
That is beyond them. They hold to a faith in Christ that
no longer corresponds to events and to history. The manner in which they had imagined the Messias is ruined by
the facts. And as yet they see nothing else. That is why
they are in total darkness. It is in the middle of this night
that the Resurrection will bring its light.

3. *The appearances of the Risen One.*

We should not think that the appearances of Christ
after His Resurrection merely give the Apostles the certitude that He is still living, that the Master is among
them and is bringing them back to the state of their relations with Him as it existed before the Passion. It is no
longer the intimacy of the days of the ministry in Galilee.
It is something else, and it is better; or rather, it is transition with a new and transformed intimacy. Just as Christ
finds life again after Easter, but a new and glorious life,
in a transformed and spiritualized body, so too the inti-

macy of the Apostles with Christ will find itself, between Easter and Pentecost, borne progressively onto a new plane, that of intimacy according to the Spirit.

It is necessary to note well the character of transition of those fifty days. No doubt, the repeated appearances of Christ up to the Ascension give the Apostles and everyone else certainty about His Resurrection. The entire faith in the mission of Christ, in His message, in His divine filiation, is built on this fact. But these manifestations of Christ have not only an apologetic scope, they have a pedagogic value, too. By means of this new presence, by means of His glorious Ascension to the right hand of the Father, by means of the Coming of the Spirit, Christ initiates His Apostles to new relationships with Him, to a spiritual intimacy, precisely that which it is proper to have with the Son of God. That is what Jesus Himself had allowed the Samaritan woman to sense. "God is spirit, and they who worship him must worship in spirit and in truth." [14] This time is one of education in the knowledge of Christ in the Spirit and in Truth.

We must recognize, as a matter of fact, certain characteristics common to all the appearances of Christ after His Resurrection. They always have something mysterious about them. Christ appears and yet people do not recognize Him right away. He is visible and in a certain way invisible. This is precisely what distinguishes this presence of the glorious Christ from His presence during the time of His life in a mortal body. The eyes of the flesh are no longer sufficient to recognize it. One needs a look illumined by faith, not in order to see Him, for

---

[14] *John* 4:24.

He is there for the eyes of the body itself, but to recognize Him, for His presence is manifested only to those
whose soul rises up to Him. All the apparitions bring,
precisely, an education, an accommodation, an illumina-
tion of this interior regard. One must learn to recognize
Christ present and hidden, the Christ Who is believed
dead and Who lives. Between the carnal look and this
presence of the glorious Christ, there is a sort of screen.
It is not a physical veil, a material impossibility. It is
truly a spiritual veil. That which creates the screen between the presence of the Risen Christ and the soul is a
certain mentality, a lack of comprehension of the plan of
God, a whole conception of the world, of a world in
which Christ is dead. They look for Christ in the world
as they conceive Him . . . and He is not there. They have
eyes in order not to see. He is there, close by, and they
are incapable of knowing it. They do not look for Him
where He is—in the world of the marvels that come
from the Father. But a word, a call, raises them to the
level of the plans of God, to the world as God sees it and
makes it; then men have to recognize Him, He is there,
present, living, triumphant. How does it come that they
have not recognized Him? They are still looking for Christ
according to what is past, in the world where He died, in
the world of before the Resurrection which is past and
out-dated, whereas He is of a new world. It is necessary
to open one's eyes to the world of the Resurrection. Such
is the profound meaning of the angel's question: "Why
do you seek the living one among the dead?" [15]

So too of Mary Magdalen, on Easter morning, the
Angels ask: "Why art thou weeping?" [16] "Woman, why

---

[15] *Luke* 24:5.
[16] *John* 20:13.

art thou weeping? Whom dost thou seek?" [17] also asks Jesus, according to His habit of asking the question which is at the very heart of the spiritual drama. No, she does not know whom she is seeking. She is looking for Jesus, . . . but Jesus according to her poor human thoughts. She is looking for Jesus Who is dead, Jesus buried. She does not find Him. This dead Jesus, this mortal Jesus, has disappeared. Yet the living Jesus is there, close, and she does not recognize Him. She is mistaken about Him, and that is why she does not recognize Him. She does not yet know Him truly in His glory of Son of God, and that is why she does not recognize Him. She takes Him for the keeper of the dead, and He is the first of the living. Still, she is looking for Him: "Tell me where thou hast laid him and I will take him away." [18] That is enough. The love of Jesus in His earthly condition prepares her to recognize Jesus in His glory. A single word enlightens her. Jesus calls her: "Mariam." She enters into the splendor of God's design. It is therefore true—He is alive. How good God is! She throws herself at His feet; she embraces Him. But Jesus gently raises her toward new horizons. It is no longer the time of the constraints of earth. Soon He will return to the Father and He will send the Spirit. Then she will really know that Jesus lives, and not only near her, but *in her*, forever. Then she will truly know Who He is—the Son of the Father, Who grants us, by His presence, to be sons in Him. "I ascend to my Father and your Father, to my God and your God." [19] Then she will finally know Christ and the Gospel He brings to the world: the news of this life beyond death which He pos-

---

[17] *John* 20:15.
[18] *John* 20:15.
[19] *John* 20:17.

sesses and gives, the news of this living presence within
our hearts. But already she knows, already she, alone in
all the world, possesses the message of joy. Let her hasten
to bring it to the Apostles, and let the good news spread
even to the extremities of the world. "Go to my brethren
and say to them . . ." [20] Yes, now she can say at last: "I
have seen the Lord." [21] She knows Christ in His power
and in His glory. The whole world is new to her.

Thus as the rising sun disperses the haze which hides
it from the sleeping earth, the Risen Christ tears away
that thick veil of Jewish and fleshly mentality which prevents His disciples from seeing Him. That is marvelously
touching in the appearance to the disciples of Emmaus.
For them too, Jesus is dead. They were hoping; it is over.
And yet Jesus is there, He walks with them on the road.
But they cannot recognize Him; they are still looking
for Him where He is not, in the world of their earthly
plans. Step by step Jesus enlightens them. Here is the
plan of God revealing itself, as well as the place, all prepared, of the suffering and triumphant Messias. This
Jesus Whom they had met so many times they had not
understood. They did not know Him. The designs of
God were infinitely more grand and more beautiful than
anything they had dreamed.

And now that they are blessing God with Him and are
nourishing themselves with this bread which He breaks
for them and with these wonders which He announces
to them, behold, they recognize Him: it is He. But already He has disappeared. And there remains only this
sweet warmth in their hearts, as the sign of an invisible

---

[20] *John* 20:17.
[21] *John* 20:18.

presence. And they have to rise up right away in order to announce the news to the Apostles and to the world.

We cannot pursue here the analysis of all the appearances of Christ. It seems that without artificially forcing things, we might recognize in all of them a common intention and similar elements. Jesus is there, living. The same and yet different. To recognize Him, it is necessary that the light of faith awake. He belongs to a new world, where only they penetrate who are able to read, through the events of this world, the mysterious plan of God. His visible presence is given back only to open souls to the presence of the invisible. We must not become attached to it avidly, carnally. We must walk at God's pace. We must foresee that He has entered into the flesh, that He has passed among us, that He has pitched His tent in this world, only in order to open to us the world to come, only in order to draw us forth, in the invisible realm, to intimacies according to the Spirit. Here we will have to attach ourselves by faith. Far from demanding the sensible presence, we must learn to go beyond it and to get along without it. "Blessed are they who have not seen, and yet have believed." [22] These are able to live with Christ. For them He is forever living, those that is, who live with this life of faith. "I will come to you . . . for I live and you shall live." [23]

Yet, if the apparitions of Christ enlighten the interior regard which permits Him to be recognized as always near and living, a decisive step remains to be taken: this regard has to be turned toward the interior. It is not enough to feel this presence of the living Christ next to us; we have to discover it within us. This ultimate illumi-

---

[22] *John* 20:29.
[23] *John* 14:19.

nation, this knowledge of Christ living in us cannot be other than the work of the Spirit Who searched the depths of God. This period of the appearances of Christ after Easter, therefore, are entirely oriented to the Feast of Pentecost which crowns it by accomplishing its mystery.

4. *Presence according to the Spirit.*

That is the profound reason why the appearances of Christ after His Resurrection all take on such a furtive and transitory character. He is not coming back in order to remain with His Apostles in a sensible and visible way. He appears in order to disappear. He appears in order to accustom them progressively to the sense of His invisible presence according to faith. This spiritual presence will always remain secondary and derived for the tastes of feeling—it is too impalpable to seem real to it. Yet we must see that it is this presence according to the Spirit which He has come to give to the world. It is not a sort of souvenir or substitute, which replaces for better or for worse, the perceptible presence of Christ, as though the presence He had come to give to the world were to disappear with His Ascension. Quite to the contrary, His historic passage on this earth during thirty-three years has prepared minds and hearts for receiving this invisible presence, in which He remains ever-living in the Church. That is the presence which He came to give to the world. It is this presence which is the most real.

Jesus Himself announced the mystery. Just as He prepared the Apostles for His Passion and His Resurrection, He disposes them and opens them to this new presence. "I speak the truth to you; it is expedient for you that I depart. For if I do not go, the Advocate will not come to you; but if I go, I will send Him to you." [24] "I will ask the Father and he will give you another Advocate to dwell with you forever, the Spirit of truth whom the world cannot receive, because it neither sees him nor knows him. But you shall know him, because he will dwell with you, and be in you. I will not leave you orphans; I will come to you." [25]

From these promises of Jesus, it stands out clearly that the presence of the Spirit in the heart will not only come to replace His personal presence, but rather to return it, to renew it in the most intimate way. "I will come to you . . . I will be with you, because I will live and you shall live." This presence is preferable to that which the Apostles have hitherto known. "It is expedient for you that I depart . . ." It is mysteriously conditional upon the departure of Jesus. His Passion effects the Redemption of the world and merits the pouring out of the Spirit on the new humanity. A new creation begins, on which the breath of God rests. Christ Himself is renewed by the vivifying Spirit: first-fruits of a new world. In His Resurrection He receives a spiritual life, seed of life for the new humanity. By His Ascension, He completes His earthly course, He ascends to the Father. The end of His mission manifests its divine origin. It is necessary for Him to have returned to the bosom of the Father in order to send the Spirit visibly; in order that the invisible mystery should visibly appear; it is from the Father and the Son, as from a single principle, that the vivifying Spirit proceeds. Thus, the whole economy of the divine

---

[24] *John* 16:7.
[25] *John* 14:16-18.

missions will have shown forth in history the invisible mystery of trinitary life.

Jesus came not only to manifest this divine life, but to give it. He communicates it in manifesting it. The work of the Incarnation is not ended with the Passion, nor with the Resurrection, but with Pentecost, in the pouring out of the Spirit. Jesus is not only He Who proceeds from the Father and returns to the Father, but also He Who, united with the Father, breathes forth the Spirit of Love and communicates their love. That is why He has come: "That they may have life and have it more abundantly." [26] This eternal life, this divine life, is knowledge of the Father in Jesus. "This is everlasting life, that they may know thee . . . and him whom thou hast sent, Jesus Christ." [27] It is the presence of the Father and of Jesus in the Spirit: "We will come to him and make our abode with him." [28]

It is participation in the life of the Father and of the Son in the Spirit. The Father manifests Himself in the Son. The Father and the Son give themselves in the Spirit, in order that the soul might possess in itself these three in one, rejoice in their presence and share in their life. United with Jesus through the Spirit, forming but one with Him, in Love, the filial soul receives everything from the Father and gives Him everything in His beloved Son.

5. Christ living in His Church.

It is this spiritual Presence, it is this eternal life that Jesus came to give the world. In it, His mission is accom-

---

[26] *John* 10:10.
[27] *John* 17:3.
[28] *John* 14:23.

plished. This Presence is ever living. Through it, the life of Christ continues in the world. Since His Resurrection, He is not only living, but life-giving. Present in the world, He penetrates it progressively with His life. That is the whole growth of the Mystical Body.

This presence of Christ in the Spirit founds the Church in unity and catholicity, for it is what gives the Apostles the courage to disperse and leave Jerusalem, in order to confront the hostile world. Had not Christ Himself promised them: "Behold I am with you all days, even to the consummation of the world"? [29] But in unity, for it is true to say that, through this divine presence, they will leave Jerusalem no more and will always be re-united in it. They leave behind this earthly and Judaic Jerusalem which is out-worn since it has rejected its Messias. But they carry with them the new Jerusalem, which rises to bear His message to the nations. They leave behind an empty and estranged Temple, but they bear within them a consecrated Temple in which the living God resides. It is the strength of God that supports them. They are carrying to the world the Word of God. The latter speaks through them; it fashions a new world. "And one night the Lord said to Paul in a vision, Do not fear, but speak and do not keep silence; because I am with thee." [30] It is this acting presence of Christ that the first Christians used to like to recognize in the martyrs. In the strictest sense, He was their strength. In the hour of combat, He it was Who fought, Who suffered, and Who triumphed in them. That is why they were so perfectly tranquil. Death itself was the coming of Christ in them and the inrushing of His life. It did not so much

[29] *Matt.* 28:20.
[30] *Acts* 18:9-10.

separate them from the world as it united them forever
to Christ Triumphant.

The outpouring of the Spirit leaves their native weakness intact but spreads in them the very presence and the
strength of the living Christ. That is what explains this
miracle of the Saints, to be at once so close to others and
so far above them, so attractive and so astonishing. But
it is not enough to say that the presence of the living
Christ helped them to found the Church, by making
them strong enough to carry everywhere the Word of
God. It is not even enough to say that it made them
marvelously eloquent, because they were speaking about
Him Whom they bore within them. We have to say that
the very thing they were carrying to the world, was the
presence of Christ within them, that it was Christ Himself, spread abroad even to the ends of the earth, that
was forming the Church.

What they were carrying around with them was not
just a discourse of wisdom, not just a manifestation of
strength; it was the Wisdom and the Strength of God,
Christ living in them. And the very experience which
they had of that in the nascent Church, made them discover in a new light, the mystery of Christ. They knew
Christ only when they gave Him. Then they understood
this folly of God, wiser than the wisdom of the learned.
They knew that Christ, rejected by His people, had become the King of the innumerable people of the Christians; they came to know that Christ Crucified was the
triumphant Head of a new creation and that the dead
Christ was giving life even to the ends of the world. They
loved the living Christ in His Church and they gave their
lives for Him.

II. THE PROGRESS OF THE CHRISTIAN
IN THE KNOWLEDGE OF JESUS CHRIST

1. *Jesus living in the Church.*

Intimacy with the living Christ in this world seems to be the privilege of the Apostles. It is this very fact which forms their unique dignity in the Church. "What we have heard, what we have seen with our eyes, what we have looked upon and our hands have handled: of the Word of Life . . . we announce to you." [31] They are the witnesses of this presence of Christ in the world.

But it is a law of divine action that what seems at first the privilege of one alone soon has to be communicated to all. He who is chosen by God is much less chosen in order to be a holder of uncommunicable benefits than he is to manifest how much the communication of these benefits presupposes a choosing of God and that this personal choice is going to become the privilege of the least among the People of God. God speaks to Abraham and to him alone, but all the faithful will one day hear the Word addressed to them alone. God consecrates David, and him alone, but one day He will make of His people an assembly of Kings. God chooses prophets for Himself, but the days will come when all will prophesy. The Word chooses a Mother for Himself, one alone, in whom He rests on this earth. "Blessed is the womb that bore thee," but even more "Blessed are they who hear the word of God and keep it." [32] Jesus chooses Apostles for Himself. He gives them His secrets so that they may

---

[31] 1 *John* 1:1-2.
[32] *Luke* 11:28.

reveal them to the world. He makes them enter into His intimacy; he unfolds before them His familiar presence, so that they might live with Him all days and participate in His mystery. Blessed are these privileged ones who have seen the Lord, who lived with Him and kept Him with them. But Jesus says to Thomas: "Blessed are they who have not seen, and yet have believed." [33]

St. Paul appears to us to be the witness par excellence of this extension of the knowledge and the intimacy of Jesus to those who did not know Him in the flesh. He is an Apostle, too; he is the Apostle par excellence. And yet he did not know Jesus at the time of His earthly pilgrimage. It is therefore because there is another knowledge of Jesus which serves to accredit the Apostle: that knowledge which he had of Him which is also knowledge according to the Spirit. More, we must say that only this spiritual knowledge of Christ is true and fecund. The other is for naught, unless it leads to this intimacy of faith. Concerning this superiority of the knowledge of Christ according to the Spirit over all earthly encounters, he gives us the ultimate formula: "Even though we have known Christ according to the flesh, yet now we know him so no longer," [34] but according to the Spirit. This we have said; the Apostles lived it before him. St. Paul adds nothing to the experience of the Apostles, but by the awareness he has of it in the light of the Spirit, he gives it a universal scope. This is the message of which he is the bearer throughout all his life, which will make him the Apostle of the pagans. Like all the Apostles, he announced the knowledge of Christ, but he announces precisely that this knowledge is not reserved to those who

---

[33] *John* 20:29.
[34] 2 *Cor.* 5:16.

were united with Christ by the bonds of blood and according to a carnal relationship, but to all those who will
be united with Him by the bonds of the Spirit in the
family of God. The highest, the most perfect, the most
profound knowledge is accessible, apart from any form
of belonging to the Jewish people, to every man, Jew or
pagan, who leaves himself open to the light of faith.
Such is His Gospel. Such is the good news he announces
to us.

For that concerns us, too. From the moment the
knowledge of Christ is no longer tied to the bonds of a
temporal meeting or a carnal kinship; it goes beyond all
the frameworks of space and time. Christ is as close to us
in the Spirit as to the first Christians, as to St. Paul, as
to the Apostles. That alone counts. He is forever the
same "heri et hodie ipse et in saecula." [35] He is always
living and life-giving, as on the first day. It is always
Easter, today and at this instant in which the Risen Lord
passes close to us.

We too must recognize Him. For us too, there is in
this a mystery to be discovered. It is not that He is far
off, but perhaps we are far from Him. He is there, but a
veil hides Him as yet from our eyes. No, it is not death
alone that will make us pass over to the other side of the
veil, but faith. St. Paul tells us: "To have Christ dwelling in your hearts through faith." [36] We must understand
this faith which gives us the knowledge of Christ living
in us, in the full sense that St. Paul gave it. It is not
merely a sort of speculative adherence to the divinity of
Christ, or even to His presence. It is a total participation,
at the price of our whole lives, in the life of Christ Him-

---

[35] *Heb*. 13:8.
[36] *Eph*., 3, 17.

self. It is an entering into Christ. Claudel's pun, according to which all "connaissance" (knowledge) is "co-naissance" (birth with) that which we understand, is valid here more than anywhere else. We must be born again. We must enter entirely into a new world, where He, living, awaits us. To take up the language of St. Paul, we must enter into His mystery.

It is only by experiencing in ourselves what Jesus first experiences in Himself, that we know what it is to live in Christ, and Who Christ, our life, is. Let us not pretend. It is only at the price of one's whole being that Christ is understood. "He who does the truth comes to the light." [37] We have to give ourselves to Christ in order to meet Him. We have to deliver ourselves to Him before He will give Himself to us. That is not a formula to be spoken. It is a life to be begun. What is more, one's whole being has to be given so that Christ may take possession of it.

But what is this mystery of Christ in which we must participate in order to know Him? It is the mystery of the Cross. It is His paschal mystery. It is the undergoing of a total stripping away of the things of this world, in order to enter into the new creation. There is no other path to discovering Jesus Christ. Has He Himself not said so? "If anyone wished to come after me, let him deny himself, and take up his cross daily, and follow me." [38] We cannot enter into the knowledge of Jesus except by participation in His mystery. We cannot enter into the mystery of Christ except by accepting His Cross.

Here we run into one of the fundamental themes of the Old Testament, that these exigencies serve to en-

[37] *John* 3:21.
[38] *Luke* 9:23.

lighten and to bring to a conclusion in Christ. One cannot see God without dying. Or again: in order to see
God, one has to die. Thus, Manue and his wife, the
future parents of Samson, who have been notified of his
birth by the angel of Yahweh, cry out: "We shall certainly die, because we have seen God." [39] Thus also Isaias,
after the vision which inaugurates his prophetic ministry: "Woe is me . . . because I am a man of unclean
lips . . . and I have seen with my eyes the King." [40] The
fundamental desire of man is to see God, but this desire
cannot be fulfilled except after death. A strange situation
is that of man, who can only enter into true life by passing through death. Christ comes to give this prophetic
presentiment its spiritual meaning and its effective realization. The death through which we have to pass is participation in His Passion. In accepting His Cross, we
enter into His mystery and finally discover Him by a
marvelous sympathy: more than that even, by a real communication of His life. That is why the intimate wish of
the human soul, which is to see God, now passes through
the Cross and ends in Christ Jesus, Who reveals to us
the Face of the Father Itself. It is this fundamental drive
of being toward the knowledge of God which becomes,
in the Christian soul, a thirst for participating fully in
the sufferings and the Passion of Christ, in order to enter
into the glory of His Resurrection and thereby, into the
knowledge of what He Himself is. What I want, says
St. Paul, is to "know him and the power of his resurrection . . . and the fellowship of his sufferings, become like
to him in death." [41]

---

[39] *Judg.* 13:22.
[40] *Is.* 6:2. Cf. *Ex.* 33:18-20. Cf. L. Bouyer, *Le sens de la vie monastique*, pp. 69-70.
[41] *Phil.* 3:11.

In this effort of the Christian toward the perfect knowledge of Christ, through participation in His mystery, the experience of the Apostles greatly enlightens us. They, first, passed through the darkness of Good Friday, in order to enter into the paschal light, in which they saw illumined the true face of the Lord. They can tell us in what this death consists through which we must pass in order to enter into intimacy with Christ.

We have seen that, for the Apostles, the crisis of Easter really has a universal bearing. With the death of Christ, everything is thrown into confusion. First of all, no doubt, the plan of their earthly lives. All that they had kept of earthly ambitions, of human viewpoints, in following Christ, are completely overturned. But far beyond what touches them personally, it is the whole plan of God for His people, and for the world, and for Christ Himself, that is put on trial. Every bit of political viewpoint that their Jewish mentality has let slide into their projects, every expectation of earthly dominance and of temporal success in the messianic salvation, has to be purified and is, in one blow, ruined. Finally, the very idea they have about the Messias is totally renewed. Their very knowledge of Christ has to be transformed. In one instant, everything disappears in total darkness. For them, a world is crumbling and they are perishing with it. The Jewish world is finished.

But everything dies in order to live again. On the ruins of these out-dated ambitions, a new world will be born again: the Church. The dead Christ will rise again and they will know Him at last, in the brilliance of His divinity. That is consistent. It is at the price of renouncing their human projects and their personal ambitions, at the price of stripping away their Jewish mentality and their collective ambitions, that they will enter into a new world where Christ is living. In His light they will discover, at last, the plan of the Father for the world and for them, the design of Redemption by the Cross. Before their eyes and in their hearts, everything has passed through death in order to be born again to true life: it is Easter. And it is the same for every Christian who enters into the mystery of Christ.

When St. Paul tells us that it is necessary to die with Christ in order to live with Christ, it is not a matter simply of a few mortifications, but of really dying, that is, of leaving this world, of being dead to the world, in order to enter into the new creation. It is a matter of dying to all our personal plans of earthly ambition, advancement, carnal satisfaction, in order that our life and our projects and our desires might no longer be from here below. As Christ Himself tells us: "They are not of the world." [42]

What the experience of the Apostles reveals to us is that our personal projects almost always insinuate themselves into a certain way of looking upon God's plan concerning the world. We elevate our personal ambitions so as to make them into projects in the Church, and we lower the Church to the level of our own ambitions. We believe that we are seeking the success of the Church, and we are seeking our own success, personal or collective, in the Church. It can happen that while working for the Church we are building up, secretly, the monument in which our self-love is sheltered. We think we are building up the Church, but this portion of the Church on which we are working becomes the pedestal

---

[42] *John* 17:16.

upon which our ambitions are raised. Secretly, we dream of a kingdom which assures us eternal benefits, all the while procuring for us earthly honors and advantages—success.

From that moment, everything is warped. For our own profit, we would like, for the Church, a triumph which would place her on the level of political societies and make us equal to the powerful of this world. We would like the action of God at the service of our ambitions. We would like Christ to assure us of a victory that would not be paid for with the sufferings and humiliations of the Cross. In a whole part of ourselves we are as yet Jews. This too-human plan which tarnishes our adherence to the Church becomes a screen between us and the presence of Christ. We would like to feel the action of Christ on behalf of the victory of our policies. And He does nothing. We look for some success. He fails us. We seek in the Church something other than Jesus and Jesus Crucified, and that is why we no longer find Him. We look for Him in a triumph that passes away; He is living in an eternal glory. To us also is the word of the Angel addressed: "Why do you seek the living one among the dead?" [43]

In order for us to discover the Risen Christ, it is necessary that our adherence pass through the crucible of His Passion. It is necessary that we be stripped of everything in order to find Him. It is necessary that we die with Christ to the world of things that pass, in which our personal project and our plans for the Church were still involving us, in order to enter with the Resurrected Christ into the world of the living, the world of the

---

[43] *Luke* 24:5.

realities that do not pass away, into the Kingdom in which He awaits us.

When we shall have thus left aside all personal ambition in the Church and every too-human ambition for the Church, then only will we see realized before our eyes the plan of God, will we receive the Church as God made her, receive our life such as God leads it, discover in each moment, in great events as in little things, the action of the Father and His very Presence. When we shall have finally allowed all the blindness of our projects and of our ambitions, personal or collective, to be dissipated, there will remain, in the transparence of history, only the disconcerting and marvelous manifestation of the presence and of the goodness of the Father. When we shall no longer seek anything except Him in the Church, we will find Jesus Christ there.

Let us listen again to St. Paul, who urges us to enter upon this total transformation of our personal lives and of our views on the Church, in order to enter into that world in which Christ lives and in which His life resurrects us. "Therefore, if you have risen with Christ, seek the things that are above, where Christ is seated at the right hand of God. Mind the things that are above, not the things that are on earth. For you have died and your life is hidden with Christ in God." [44] ". . . you have died with Christ to the elements of the world . . ." [45] "Therefore, as you have received Jesus Christ Our Lord, so walk in him." [46] "Strip off the old man with his deeds and put on the new, one that is being renewed unto perfect knowledge 'according to the

---

[44] *Col.* 3:1-3.
[45] *Col.* 2:20.
[46] *Col.* 2:6.

image of his Creator.' Here there is not 'Gentile and Jew' . . . but Christ is all things and in all." [47]

2. *The Eucharistic Christ.*

If we have participated with the Apostles in the Passion and the Death of Christ, we are prepared truly to discover Him. But if we seek the living Christ, it is in the Eucharist that we find Him, He is there, resurrected, and ready to communicate His life to us. The close presence of Christ in the Eucharist is for us what the appearances of the Risen Christ were for the Apostles. The Eucharist is the very manifestation of Jesus Resurrected in His Church. It is the presence of Jesus spread abroad even to the ends of the world. It is the life of Jesus, now incorruptible, diffused even to the end of time. In short, it is Jesus Himself given to all and to each. It is He as He must be in the world—the Son of God everywhere present, everywhere given, infinite love, heart of a new world Who propels the charity of God through all the members of humanity and vivifies the entire Body, for the praise of the Father.

All the characteristics so peculiar to the appearances of Jesus to His Apostles we find again in this Eucharistic manifestation. Here He is once more visible and invisible. He gives a sign of His presence. Yet the soul which has not yet risen to the world of faith does not recognize Him—it grasps nothing. It moves in a world of appearances in which the living Christ escapes it. It is living in the world of darkness and of death.

The presence of Christ in the Eucharist calls forth and

---

[47] *Col.* 3:9-11.

demands faith. It is entirely a drawing out of faith. It accustoms us to moving in this invisible world, where the Risen Christ reigns. Here, in this new light, in this supernatural world, is Jesus present; here is Christ living and giving life, the Lamb immolated for the sins of the world become the source of Redemption for all God's people.

Thus the Eucharistic presence draws us to the exercise of faith, accustoms us to discovering Christ with the eyes of faith. But that is not all. Just as we have seen, regarding the manifestations of the Risen Christ between Easter and Pentecost, the gift of the Eucharistic Christ accustoms us progressively to an interiorizing of the presence of Christ; it is no longer outside that we must look for Him, it is within. "Christ dwells by faith in your hearts." In a marvelous way, the divine pedagogy of the Eucharistic Sacrament invites us to turn our eyes within and teaches us to find Jesus in the deepest intimacy of the heart. If we may thus express ourselves, it is the Sacrament, the efficacious sign of the interiorizing of the knowledge of Christ. The very act of sacramental reception shows us Christ before us, near us, the Christ of the Gospel, His gestures and His voice, and the gift of Himself which He makes to us through His holy and venerable hands. But the presence of the Christ of the Gospel ends in us. The term of His work is in the center of the heart. He Whom we have known as it were from the outside, is there in the inmost depths. He Whom we have known by history, is there actual and living. The final act of Him Whose actions we have all itemized, is to come to us. He Whom I have known from afar, *ecce*, He is here, close by, He is there within me.

This passing of Christ into the inmost soul is not, as

some people like to say at times, a visit. It is rather more
of a dwelling; even more, a life in common. This too the
Eucharistic sign expresses in a marvelous and inexhaustible way. Christ has come as the food of the soul. He is
there within us, in order to live there and to transform us
into Himself. He does not come just to go away again,
He comes to stay. He comes to live with us during the
whole day of life, and in order that we might live it with
Him. He comes in order to draw us into His life. To
enter into the Eucharistic mystery is to live habitually
with Christ; it is to spend one's life with Him. "He who
eats my flesh and drinks by blood, abides in me and I in
him." [48]

Let us note this fact: here, in our heart, is the one
true place of repose for Christ. When He comes to earth,
when He manifests Himself in the flesh, St. John uses
the words which designate a passing presence and a
transitory dwelling-place: "The Word was made flesh,
and dwelt among us." [49] It is a Pasch, a passage of the
Lord. When He comes into our hearts, He rests, dwells
and so to speak, installs Himself there for eternity.
"*Manet.*" For it is here that begins what shall never end.
For this life which He gives to our souls, is His life,
which does not pass away—Eternal Life.

Strange as it may seem, this interiorizing of the seeking of Christ, far from shrinking up the Christian life
into an individualistic attitude, opens it up to the com-
munitary sense. What the Eucharist gives us and shows
us is Christ present to all. Communion is a common
union. All together receive Christ and bear Him in themselves. That is part of its sacramental scope. It represents

---

[48] John 6:57.
[49] John 1:14. Note: The original Greek has "pitched his tent" here.

and effects Christ present in us, on the condition that we not give this "us" the narrow meaning of a particular group, but that we see it as the very expression of the Christian community. That which appears as a sign and that which is in reality, is Christ given to each and present in all; it is the presence of the Risen Christ in the Christian Assembly. The Eucharist reveals to us Christ living in us. It signifies and carries out the living and beloved presence of Christ in His Church. It forms the Church by this very presence and by this common love. It is the Sacrament of the Mystical Body.

But what the Eucharistic Sacrament teaches us above all is that this access to the intimacy of Jesus living in the Church, can be given us only through our entering into the mystery of the Cross. The facts are there. The sacramental sign is clear: we receive Jesus in our hearts only through participation in the Sacrifice of the Mass, and through the Mass, in the Cross. That means, once again and in a very precise way, that on the sacramental level, we can have access to Jesus present in us only if we participate first in the Mystery of His death and of His Resurrection.

We have mentioned what the profound demands were, in our personal life and in our life in the Church, for this dying with Christ. A whole world has to be left behind, in order to enter a new world in which Christ is living and life-giving.

It is enough to say here that the Mass is really the Sacrament of this dying with Christ, or more exactly, of this passing into life with Christ. For it is precisely in this regard that it appears most clearly that the Mass is not only the memorial of the Death of Christ, as is sometimes said; but much more, the memorial of His passing through death to the true life. We have to give the Passion of Christ, as it is commemorated through the Mass, all its dimensions. With Christ and in Him, in the hour of Friday darkness, a whole world crumbles and dies. It is the world of death, apparently victorious, that engulfs Christ Himself. "This is your hour, and the power of darkness." [50] But this death of Christ accepted out of love, is the victory of Christ over the world. He triumphs over the powers of death that enchain the world. He pushes the world of sin back into the past, into the "outdated". This world is finished; its power vanquished. It is the death of death.

From that time forward a new era opens in history. A new world begins. What is present is the living Christ and the universe to which He communicates His life. Thus in the Mass, the commemoration of the mystery of Christ is not achieved in the Consecration of bread into His Body, and of wine into His Blood, which recall His passion and death. It is achieved in the Communion, which is the presence of Christ beyond death, of the Risen Christ. He Who was believed dead lives and gives life to the world.

The Christian who participates in the Eucharistic Christ enters at the same time into all the riches of His mysteries. He dies with Christ. He participates in His Passion and in His Cross, and for him, a whole world is disappearing, to which he too is disappearing—the whole world of ambitions, of rivalries and of hatreds, the world of sin and death. This world is passé for him: ". . . world dead and crucified for him," to which He Himself is also dead and crucified. But at the same time he enters a

---

[50] *Luke* 22:53.

new world, a world of Resurrection and of Life. It is
here that he meets the living Christ. Just as he has shared
in His death, he shares in His Resurrection. From the
Risen Christ he receives a new life, a life which is no
longer subject to death, "life at last, the real life." It is
not enough to say that he receives the life of Christ; he
gives it to them. With Him and in Him, he is dead and
living and life-giving for all. For Christ Himself is his
life and in Him he gives himself to the Church forever.
That is why he has already passed into the eternal. Death
so to speak, no longer has any hold on him. It will take
only that which he has already long since given. "O
death, where is thy victory? O death, where is thy
sting?" [51] It can do nothing to the Christian who has
found Christ, for with St. Paul he can say: "For me to
live is Christ, and to die is gain." [52]

3. *He Who is to come.*

Nevertheless we must recognize that there remains a
final stage for us to pass through in order ultimately to
rejoin the living Christ. More exactly, the soul which
already possesses in itself the living Christ, in its pro-
foundest depths, awaits in the darkness of faith that final
call by which Christ invites it to throw itself into His
arms: "Media nocte clamor factus est: ecce sponsus
venit: exite obviam ei." [53] Here, each soul represents in
itself the mystery of the Church. For it is the entire
Church which possesses Christ in herself and which
awaits in the night of this present world the Dawn of

---

[51] 1 *Cor.* 15:55.
[52] *Phil.* 1:21.
[53] *Matt.* 25:6.

that blessed Day in which Christ will appear in her, triumphant, in order to fulfill time in eternity.

Here again the Eucharist becomes the Sacrament of our awaiting. There is no doubt that in sacramentally renewing for us the Passion of Christ, it is reminding us that the world of sin and of death is finally overtaken and buried with Him. In giving us Christ living and life-giving, it introduces us into a new world, into a resurrected world where life dies no more. But it introduces us there with our eyes closed. The realities which surround and penetrate us are as yet invisible. Christ Jesus is there living in us, living in the Christian assembly, but we have not yet seen His face. A new world is forming, the foretaste and pledge of which we have in our soul, but the eye has not yet seen, the ear has not yet heard, and the heart has not yet tasted that joy of Resurrection which God prepares for His elect.

And we ourselves, finally, in this renovated world, are to appear as God desires us in Jesus from the origin of the world and in such wise that the image of the Father and His life might be forever accomplished in us, under the breath of the Spirit of the Son. But we ourselves do not know what we are to be. Our new face has not yet appeared to us; it will be revealed to us only in the effulgence of the glory of the only-begotten Son.

That is why, in celebrating the Holy Eucharist, we at once possess and desire Christ. We desire to know at last, in the light of glory, Him Whom we possess, living, in the darkness of faith. But this gift of Himself which He makes to us, beneath the eucharistic veils, is for us a pledge and an assurance of this return of Christ and of the coming of His glory. "Futurae gloriae nobis pignus datur." [54] The gifts of God are without repentance. If He gives Himself today, it is not just so as to take Himself back; it is rather to reveal to us, beneath the sign of the Sacrament, in the darkness of faith, what the reality of His gift will be on the great day of His return. In receiving the Host, already I bear the foretaste and the pledge of that ultimate presence through which the living and glorious Christ will be eternally all in all, to draw His whole Church, assembled from the four corners of the world, into the impetus of His filial love, toward the Father, in an eternal Eucharist. That is why, each time that I accomplish this mystery in time, I am announcing, I am expecting and I am preparing its eternal fulfilment: "For as often as you shall eat this bread and drink the cup, you proclaim the death of the Lord, until he comes." [55]

In the Eucharist, participating with my whole being, with the entire Church, in the passing of Christ through death in order to enter into His glory, I am aspiring unflaggingly toward the day when Christ will come to get me, and to that Day among days when He will come to get His Church, in order to make us pass from this mortal world into the renewed universe in which will appear at last that divine Face which will constitute our joy for all eternity. "Veni Domine Jesu. Etiam venio cito. Amen." [56]

---

[54] Office of St. Thomas for the Feat of Corpus Christi.
[55] 1 *Cor.* 11:26.
[56] *Apoc.* 22:20.

6

CHURCH VIRTUES

ONE COMES AWAY astonished, upon rereading most of the books on spirituality of the last century, at the small place given therein to the social influence of the Christian life. The itinerary of the soul to God is described throughout as an individual effort. Conversion, active and passive purifications, contemplation are considered as stages of the relationship of the soul with God. The Christian virtues are studied in their nature and in their progression. Yet, not one chapter on the necessity of letting one's faith radiate in the apostolate, not one on the duty of being responsible for the conditions of life in the circle of the family, the neighborhood or the job, not one on the demands for services to be rendered to the Church in the framework of the parish or of movements, or on the concrete demands of international charity and of the organization of peace, or on the missionary duty of every Christian and his active participation in the communal liturgical life. It seems that the life of grace and the organism of the virtues have been understood only in the individual Christian. More and more we feel that it is necessary to see them rooted in a community, developing through it and for it—and not just Christian virtues, but Church virtues.

1. *The Christian virtues belong to the Church.*

Catholic Action has made us take a definite step toward discovering the true dimensions of our Christian vocation. Grace does not develop in individuals separated from the rest of the world, as in a laboratory experiment. It transforms our life just as it is, that is to say, taken up entirely in the "milieux" in which we are. Man is a living part of the family, of the working environment, of the community, of humanity. He is father or mother, American or Chinese, of the 20th century, not of the Middle Ages. Grace takes him just as he is. In him, the milieux of which he is a part are aimed at and attained. The spiritual life is then not only a meeting of the soul with God, but a new way of living, of reacting, in the environments of which we are a part, in order to make the influence of grace pass into them. It is a meeting of God with the world which passes through us. A difficult task, for it presupposes not only good personal resolutions, but a more vivid realization of the opposition of the world of which we are to the demands of the Gospel, an incessant struggle, a pressure, an action from within to implant by every channel, institutions which are according to justice and relationships that operate in charity.

The Christian is called upon to meet the world—that which lives, that which works, that which makes history. He faces up to it; he has difficulties; he has failures; perhaps he makes mistakes. But he brings something, he serves, he enlightens, he is the light, he is the salt, he is the leaven. Only then, and in the very effort to carry the life of Christ to the world, he knows what it is to be a Christian, and that it is not easy.

Yet, we are still far from having understood completely to what extent each Christian is one, in all his spiritual life, with all other Christians, and ultimately, with all other men and with the world in its total history.

We have especially emphasized how the Christian or the militant belongs to definite environments: family, profession, neighborhood; how they have to accept a Christian conscience and responsibility for these environments—to work with others to modify the structures, to create institutions, to bring about a climate which will render the Christian life possible and desirable. Pressing and innumerable tasks which fall to Catholic Action—all that is necessary.

We would like to show here that these tasks are caught up in a larger whole which conditions them. The Christian is situated in a family by his birth, in a nation by his ancestry, in a profession and a community by his temporal actions . . . and he is responsible for these. He is one with these human fabrics of which he is a part and this solidarity must move toward a work of Redemption. That is true.

But by his spiritual birth, by his Baptism, the Christian is born into the Church. He is of her, in the strongest sense of the word. He has received in her and through her his being of grace, just as he was born of a human family and received from it his carnal being. He is born of the Church. He is son and member of the Church. Henceforth, the Christian is not only one with the human environments in which he finds himself involved;

he is also one with the Church of which he is a living part. That too, that above all, has immense repercussions on his whole spiritual life.

We feel more and more this Church-ly aspect of our Christian life, with the concrete demands this implies for the spiritual life. In effect, we have to say that not only is the Christian responsible for the milieux in which he lives, but that he is also responsible for the Church herself, in his way, as a layman or as a cleric, but always in a real sense. That is to say that it is important for him to know not only whether the human environments of which he is a part are disposed to receive the Gospel, but also whether the Church is ready to bring it. That in part depends upon him.

That is much more demanding than we might believe. For the evangelization of the world depends not only on what the Church does, but on what she is. It is not enough for her to announce Christ; she must live of Him in order to bring Him to the world. Thus each member of the Church has his place and according to his mission, as Christian, as a militant, as a priest or as a Bishop, must see to it, insofar as it depends on him, that the Church expresses before the world the face of Christ and His love. This is the most important thing of all. For ultimately God does not save the world by means of a man, nor by means of a movement, nor by means of a Congregation or an Order, separately, but by means of the Church, the Mystical Body of Christ.

It is therefore not enough that through Catholic Action each human milieu should find responsible Christians to think it out and organize it, in order to lay it open to the action of grace. It is not enough that human relations become conductors of the Charity of Christ and of His light. It is not enough that Christians become aware of the social proportions of their life of grace in the human environments of which they are part and form movements adapted to these environments.

It is also, it is above all, necessary that they become aware of their Church responsibility, that they should feel themselves at once linked with the world and linked with her in this precise point of the world, in this instant of history in which their life engages them. They are charged not only with acting on the world in order to bring it to Christ, but also with acting in the Church, with all the others, in order that she should remain living and catholic; that she might keep in her features the purity of the Gospel, and that she might become at last more and more adapted for bringing her message to the world.

There is no true Christian, no militant, no priest, who has not this double fidelity to the world to be evangelized and to the Church which evangelizes. In truth, there is no double fidelity, but one sole fidelity—fidelity to grace. For that is precisely what we have to understand. Grace has been given us for the Church and in her, in such wise that the life of grace, the growth of the spiritual life, the very purification of the soul, cannot be accomplished except in her and through our insertion into the Church for the salvation of the world. It is precisely by responding in the most exact way possible to the actual demands of the life of the Church, to the movement of the Spirit in her, to her actual adaptation to the evangelization of the world, that the Christian receives the fulness of his grace, responds fully to his vocation and becomes a saint.

That involves a very important consequence, namely,

that one is not a saint in the same way in all ages. Grace is given us in the Church and for her. The Church lives by the divine life which is eternal, but in order to bring it to the world which changes. In her, the Incarnation continues and the eternal is introduced into time. That is why the eternal dispositions of the Church will be adapted in each Christian, in each group, each order, each movement, to the necessities of an epoch, to the call of the times. We have to consider the Christian virtues according to what is eternal in them, and according to what is imposed in every age. But also we must look to see in what actual way the life of the Church demands that we adapt these virtues to the needs of our time. That implies a profound sense of the Church and of her mission. By the Christian life, which is apostolic, we are engaged in such a way in the Church that we follow the very rhythm of her life. Grace acts in us, for the development of the Body of Christ, according to the exigencies of her growth.

In every age there is a new way for the Christian in the Church to be at odds with the world in what it contains that is evil, and to live in the world in what it contains that is good. It is this dying to the world in order to love God according to the very needs and, so to speak, the rhythm of the life of the Church in one's time that is the most profound law of the development of Christian life and virtues. The final demand of the life of the Christian, the most intimate purification of his soul and of his apostolate, is to be given over, in the Church, to the powerful action of God. It is to accept to die with her, in order to be reborn with her. It is to enter with and through her into the paschal mystery.

2. *The Christian virtues build up the Church.*

Our research must therefore lead us to a better understanding of how the actual development of the life of the Church has to draw the Christian along in its rhythm, and impose upon him the purifying law of her spiritual growth.

As the basis of everything, we must put the great intuition of St. Paul. God has seen us, has wanted us, has loved us before the origins of the world for His Son, Jesus Christ, and for the constitution in time of His Mystical Body, which is the Church. He chose us, He has given us grace and life, He wants us to be saints not for ourselves but for that great Whole of which we are the parts. "He chose us in him before the foundation of the world that we should be holy . . . in love." [1] That is why grace is given to each of us as members of the Mystical Body, with regard to the life of the whole Body. The gifts of God are apportioned out to us, not for our personal profit, but for that of the whole. The most profound rhythm of our spiritual life is to be in accord, put in harmony with and, as it were, fused into the life of the Whole Christ. The development of our life will make us become more and more aware of this quality of members of Christ, and its perfection will be to consent to it fully in order to give all that we are and to receive the influence of the whole of the Body. To be fully in accord with the life of the Church, to be fully of the Church, is to be a saint. "To each one of us grace was given according to the measure of Christ's bestowal . . .

---

[1] *Eph.* 1:4.

in order to perfect the saints for a work of ministry, for building up the body of Christ." [2] This perspective of the whole dominates the entire development of the spiritual life. It does not concern only the charisms of which St. Paul is especially speaking here, but all the graces that are given us for the building up of the Mystical Body of Christ.

Throughout all the history of the world God is pursuing only one thing: the completion of His Church. The history of the world under the guidance of Providence pursues a single goal which is the building up of the Mystical Body of Christ. It is only that which gives it meaning, a goal, and a significance. Otherwise it is only incoherence. It is this alone which is made to finish history: sacred history, the plan of God.

But this completion of the Church contains, so to speak, two aspects: it is at once the completing of her extension and the completing of her purity, the progressive fulfilment of her catholicity and the deepening of her holiness. Providential action works without cease in building up the Church in these two dimensions.

The whole development of humanity, the whole unfolding of history, the whole blossoming of civilizations, permit the Church to grow in the world and to manifest the inexhaustible riches of the grace of Christ. Everything that happens in the world, all the wealth of thought and the splendors of art, the discoveries of the spirit and the movements of peoples, the entire unreeling of history, all that is for Him.

Yet this progressive extension of the Mystical Body of Christ through which it tends to catholicity does not

---

[2] *Eph.* 4:7-12.

suffice to define its progress. That internal development of the Church whereby she penetrates with divine grace all human riches, baptizes all civilizations, assimilates and saves in herself all the products of the mind and of art, is not enough to define the plan of God for her. For, at the same time, she penetrates the world and is detached from it. She becomes more catholic and she becomes more holy. She gets involved in earthly realities, but in order to draw them to heaven. She unfolds in time, but only in order to finish in eternity. That is her mystery.

The Epistle to the Ephesians shows us Christ Who loves the Church by delivering Himself up for her in order to sanctify her. Throughout history He pursues this work of Redemption. Through all events, all cataclysms, all persecutions, He continues unflaggingly this unique design which is to purify His Church in order that, St. Paul tells us, He might present her to Himself "in all her glory, not having spot or wrinkle or any such thing, but that she might be holy and without blemish." [3] That is one of the keys to history.

Where we perhaps see only a catastrophe, God sees the purification of His Church. Where everything seems to us to be thrown into doubt, it is perhaps just that some new progress is in preparation. For as utopian as it is to establish a sort of myth of progress according to which mankind would be necessarily proceeding to the amelioration of its lot by means of man's resources, it is equally correct to think that the Church develops like a living thing. By means of profound sloughing-offs, which are conditioned by the becoming of the world and

---

[3] *Eph.* 5:27.

the great revolutions which agitate it, she realizes more and more purely her divine calling; she responds to the design of God for her; she becomes what she has to be: the Spouse of Christ ready to leave for the Eternal Wedding.

That is why the Church is as it were doubly tied to human history. The Incarnation is continued in time. Each epoch, each country, each discovery demands from the Church an appropriate reaction for seizing, through her saints, that which can be assumed into Christ. Each age of mankind, each century of history, each human pulsation calls forth in the Church a movement of the Spirit which takes it up and divinizes it, in order to complete in it the Mystery of the Incarnate Word. It is not enough to say that she must be of her time; she is this very time insofar as it bears fruit in the total Christ. In order to live, she has to be actual.

In order that the Church might live, it is necessary that Christians stand in the present. Nowadays we have a better perception of how necessary that is. People readily have the impression of a sort of delay on the part of the Church as regards human development. A new world has developed, rich in inventions, in techniques, in organs of influence, and the Church was not there. This world has provided men, and they are no longer Christians. We get the impression that in certain ages Christians scarcely viewed the renewal of the Church except in the sense of a return to the past and to forms of life that had changed. It is necessary and sound to face up to the facts and to bear Christ to the world such as it is. To return to the sources of faith and of grace, to have the sense of their eternal value, is to have the sense of their immediacy, of their possibility for revealing new riches in face of all historical circumstances. The eternal is not the past; it is the present.

This lack of adaptation, this bankruptcy of immediate reaction in the face of the problems of the age has come about in the Church, partly because of the lack of initiative of the laity. They were for a long time more passive than active. Their role seems precisely to be to place the action of the Church into contact with the realities of the world. The Church is the Mediatrix of divine life. But in the Church the Hierarchy transmits the grace of Christ to the Church organism, the laity make this divine life penetrate into all the machinery of the world's life. That is why, normally, the laity will have, more than the clergy, the sense of the adaptations and the creations needed for the Church to respond to the needs of her times.

It is therefore essential to the life of the Church that all together, clergy and laity, each in its role, in close contact with the very evolution of the life of the world, take pains to make penetrate therein the effulgence of the grace which is in the Church, in order to establish all things in Christ. It is the present whose return to the Father we are charged with; we must be part of it, or we are not truly in the current of grace.

But in the name of sanctity also, the Church must be of her times. She achieves in herself the Redemption of the world. She meets in every age not only the wealth of the world but its sin. She has to assume in a constantly new way everything that is good, but she must also make a break, in a renewed and adapted way, with the evil which is being transformed. She suffers from evil, she bears the sin of the world, she expiates. She is betrayed, she is handed over, she is judged, she is scourged and she is crowned with thorns, she is crucified. All the powers of evil have allied themselves against her; in each age these become renewed and take on more insidious forms.

Each age offers to the Church by means of its very difficulties an occasion of Redemption and of holiness. We must not let it pass. At each moment of her history, the Church plunges into that regenerating bath of tribulation, into that baptism of blood from which she emerges more pure, more beautiful, more holy than ever. The entire history of the world is on the march not only in order to enrich the Church, but in order to purify her.

That concerns each one of us. We have said that grace is given to us to participate in the life of the Church. We are called, each one in his place and in his moment, to complete in the Church the mystery of Incarnation and of Redemption. Virtues are given to us in order to permit us by grace to pursue in ourselves the mystery of Christ. They allow us the necessary reactions in order to go beyond and to assume that which happens in time, to arise toward God while walking on the earth. In that, they sanctify us. But in ourselves, it is the whole Church which is on the march to her goal, so that through these (reactions) it is the Church that sanctifies herself.

That is why it is essential for our Christian life to be adapted to our times. We have the duty of being, within the Church, of our time. As Father de Montcheuil used to say: "The soul must not isolate its spiritual efforts from the historical religious movement which conditions them." Or again, as M. O. Culmann writes: "It is important that the believer live in the present, the role of which in history is determined in a precise way." [4]

---

[4] O. Culmann, Le Christ et le Temps, p. 53.

It is not enough for us to be told that we have to practice virtues at all times; we have to be told how to practice them in our times. The great orientations are the
same, the ways of carrying them out are different. The inspiration is unique, the expression changes. That is why,
though it is always good to share in the spirit which
animates the lives of the saints, it might be dangerous
to reproduce literally what they did in another age. It
is the same Charity, the same truth, the same justice,
the same respect, but they are not expressed in the same
way in the Middle Ages and in the 20th Century. The
progress of the world demands of us a renovation of love.

In order to be a saint, the Christian must accept the
sufferings and detachments that Christ demands of His
Church. His personal detachment enters into the collective renunciations, which impose upon it their meaning and their historic scope.

Not only does his action in this way serve the external
development of the Church in her visible structures, but
his passion serves her even more in her intimate life. It
is not only when he is working, but when he is suffering
that he is developing and sanctifying her. The highest
collaboration of the Christian with the life of the Church
is his perfect availability, his loving passivity under the
action of God. In that he receives for himself and for the
Church of which he is a part the highest and most delicate impulses of the Spirit of God.

But it also and especially his insertion into the Church
which opens him to the action of grace. It is for this
that God is working in him. It is through His providential action, which at each period of her history purifies
the Church, that the Christian himself is purified and
sanctified in her. Therefore he has to discern at each

moment what is the appeal that God is causing His Church to hear in order to enter into it himself with his whole being. He has to know, by means of the interior counsel of the Spirit which animates her, and by the external directives of the Hierarchy which governs her, what are the actual demands of the life of the Church, what are the detachments that God expects of her in order to fulfill them in himself, what are the sufferings that she is undergoing in order to offer them with her, what are the sins of the world which she bears, in order to expiate them with her. It is only at this price, through this full insertion into history, through this complete adaptation to the actual needs of the Church that the Christian will render fruitful the grace which is given him. He will have to give himself to the action of God on His Church in order to see where He is leading her and in order to consent to her movement.

Only then will he be really responding to the needs of the world. Only then will he be truly of his time, because he will be leading it to the term to which it secretly tends. Only then will he be responding to the needs of the Church by completing in himself what is lacking still to the Passion of Christ for her sake.

3. *Our virtues engage the Church.*

For we have to realize that if our whole life is engaged in the Church, our action also engages the Church. We depend on the Church, but in a certain way the Church depends on us. We are purified in the Church, but our consent and our giving purify the Church. Because we are truly part of the Church, our actions compromise her.

That is especially true for the clergy, priests and

Bishops, religious men and women. They are more particularly of the Church and they represent her more in
the eyes of the world. Because the Church is holy, we
must not believe that everything in the Church is holy.
We have the certitude that her Spouse will never
abandon her. But we have received neither the certitude
nor the promise that all the members of the Church will
constantly be animated by the Spirit of Jesus. We know
that all can sin. But what is worse is that they can remove themselves from Christ not only in their ordinary—
and if we may say private—lives, but also at the very
moment when they act as representatives of the Church,
when they are exercising Church activities, when they
are making the Church act. There are therefore activities
of the Church, ecclesiastical actions, which can no longer
be quickened by the spirit of the Gospel. These deformations, if they become collective, risk hardening into
customs and finally institutions. They therefore disfigure
in an atrocious way the visage of the Church. In such or
such a one of its parts, the Body of Christ lives no more
of the Spirit of Christ. It is deformed. We do not recognize it any more. In this way are born divisions and
schisms.

Let us admit it, a spirituality that is too individualistic can thus deform conscience. We are accustomed to
examining ourselves solely on our private lives; it is with
difficulty that we feel ourselves responsible for the ways
of acting, the attitudes of the group or of the portion of
the Church of which we have charge. It is possible to accept not only the law, but also the counsels for oneself,
on a personal basis, and be far from the evangelical spirit
on a collective basis. It is not chimerical to think that a
pastor detached from money for himself, may be exces-

sively preoccupied with gain for his parish and his works. That will influence his pastoral attitudes. These things compromise and involve the Church. It is not inconceivable that superiors, having taken the vow of poverty for themselves, should not practice poverty, generosity and abandonment with regard to their house and their congregation. That can be true for a certain collective pride, for the desire of domination and for any one at all of the capital sins. We renounce it for ourselves; we find it again in the group. A deformation all the more grave to the extent that a certain personal detachment hides from the conscience a collective attachment which may be nothing more than a transference of basic cupidity. The root has not been removed. It will not be until it shall have been extirpated from the group. Deformations all the more distressing in that they attack the Church herself and compromise her influence. She who was supposed to bear witness collectively, by her very structure and her social life, to disinterestedness and love, seems in this or that part involved in the bonds of greed and of the ambitions of the world. She who was supposed to bear the Spirit of Christ and of His Gospel seems in this particular portion animated by the spirit of the world. Who is to say that we have not at times suffered from these attitudes acquired in time which mask from the world the eternal face of Christ which is to shine forth in His Church!

We must ask ourselves incessantly with regard to each of the Christian virtues, with regard to detachment and humility, with regard to justice and respect for persons, with regard to the love of all men and of pardon for injuries, not only whether we practice them in our own personal name, but if we practice them in the Church, if we make this particular part of the Church for which we are responsible practice them. It is necessary that the Church herself become, through us, in the part for which we are responsible, poor and gentle, humble, peaceful, benevolent and beneficent, so that the face of Jesus Christ Himself might shine forth in her. May the breath of the Beatitudes, may the evangelical spirit penetrate our lives and hers, may our virtues be Church virtues!

Not that we claim this is new . . . and that we have to bring the spirit of Christ to the Church. A vain claim, that. Where else would we get it except in her? We could only bring our own spirit and create a schism. But we are well aware that what is begun is never finished. The Spirit which we have received in the Church must still be passed on in her until the end of time, in order that she may give it to the world. That is the condition of her adaptation. For that which makes this or that portion of the Church unadapted to its role, is precisely the weight of a too-human past, the hardening and the relapse of researches that are too human, of attitudes that are too human.

All this is true of the clergy but also of the laity. They too represent the Church, as Christians, and sometimes they act in the name of the Church. They are less officially the Church than the clergy, but they are more in contact with everything. That is why they are realizing that more and more, the whole of their action engages and modifies the Church. Finally, it is on the attitude of Christians that people will judge the Church. What the world demands of us in order to be completely adapted to it, is nothing more than the purity of the Gospel. The latter is always actual because it is eternal.

So that we are brought back to the Gospel, we are

invited to evangelical purity at once from within, by the very life of the Church which is continuously rising upward, by the demand for sanctity which is renewed in her, and from the outside, through the call of the world which demands, in order to believe, that we be saints.

In order to be fully in the current of grace, it is necessary for us to place ourselves, according to our own situation, exactly at this point of contact between the Church and the world. In order to hear the call which the world addresses to the Church; in order to grasp the answer that the Spirit suggests to her and into which we have to enter in order for it to be pronounced; in order to respond to our vocation, we must enter into the spiritual effort that the Spirit suggests to the Church to save the world of today.

4. *The Church sustains our virtues.*

It is true to say that our virtues support the Church and assure her progress and her purification. It is even truer to say that the Church supports our virtues and insures our progress and our sanctification. The good state of each of the members concurs to the health of the body; but it is the life of the body which assures the integrity of the members and their unity. In this sense also, our Christian virtues possess their total structure and their full value only in the Body of Christ. They are in reality the disposition of each member which joins it with the whole of the Body; they belong to the Church; they are Church virtues.

We might first of all point out a certain number of dispositions that are especially necessary for the Christian in order for him to accomplish his functions and to hold his place in the Church: obedience, to accept the orders of the leaders; fraternal charity to get along with others; zeal, to promote the good of the Church. We might arrive then to a definition along those lines of a certain number of ecclesiastical virtues.

But we would soon have to note that this would be completely inadequate. In truth, it is not some particular virtues which assure the good conduct of the Christian and of the cleric in the Church, but all the virtues which are necessary to the life of the Church and which, taken in themselves, have a Church sense. Perhaps it has not been emphasized enough: all the virtues have their root in the life of the Church and must bear fruit for her. They are based on her development.

This ignorance of the Church character of life and of the Christian virtues, is no doubt the basic reason why people have more or less confounded the Church with the ecclesiastical Hierarchy alone, and that they have not viewed her in the dimensions of the Body of Christ and of her action in the world. While it is true that his dispositions toward the Hierarchy are essential in the life of the Christian, it is also true that his life in the Church is not reduced to that. It requires bonds not only with the Head but also with the other members and with the external world. All these supernatural virtues are at the service of Christ living in the Church for the purpose of saving the world.

This aspect must be emphasized, especially as regards the theological virtues. It would be too easy to believe that only moral dispositions have a social bearing and are to be lived in the Church. The theological dispositions are in the first place sustained, lived and expanded in the Church and through her. Let us, for example, consider what our Hope is. We know very well that its personal aspect is fundamental: we hope for God from God for ourselves. But we also know and we feel more and more, the social proportions of our Hope. We cannot hope for and desire a solitary salvation. We expect from God the salvation of the world. We hope for the fulfilment of the promises. What promises? Those which have been made to His people and renewed to the Church.

Truly, our Hope is the very hope of the Church. We await with her that return of Christ which will be the glorification of His Church, the final outpouring of His grace on her and through her, on the world. We await, in the Church, the triumph of the Church, and the expectation of our personal salvation has no support, no meaning, no solidity, apart from this light. We hope for our salvation as members of the People of God, and we wait for it in the expectation of the Church which hopes for Christ.

It is in this total perspective, and through their very insertion in the Church, that we are permitted to grasp the profound meaning, the dynamism of all the Christian virtues. They are at once the personal dispositions of the Christian and the articulations of the Mystical Body, the common dispositions of the People of God in its march toward the Promised Land.

This march has its tempo. The virtues make us walk at the Church's pace. We must in fact come to that central point from which everything flows and where is formed unity. It is through the mediation of the Church that all the virtues join up to make us participate in the mystery of Christ, and to make us participate in the mystery of the world insofar as it has to be transformed by Christ. They are, within the Christian and within the Church, that juncture-point, that link, that joining of human life and divine life, of the forces which come from below and the gifts which come from above, of the temporal and the eternal. They achieve, they continue, they pursue through us in the Church, the Mystery of the Incarnation. They enter the world whence we are, in order to make penetrate the life of God that we have received. For we may analyze each virtue according to its proper object, but the whole of the Christian virtues aims to effect in us, at a single stroke, that death to the sinful world and entrance into the new life which are the blossoming of the grace received at Baptism. To die in order to live, that is the entire meaning of the dynamism of the virtues, which unites us to the very Mystery of Christ, to His Cross, to His Resurrection, to His Pasch, to His going to the Father. But this same rhythm of death for life, essential to Christian progress, is not independent of our life in the Church. It is not just a personal rhythm; it is a collective rhythm. It is the very striving of God's people. It is formed in the desert, it is united with the Cross, it is fulfilled in the Eucharist.

It is not indeed a matter of dying to the world in the abstract, but in history. It is a matter of entering, all together this very day, into that Passion which the world causes Christ and His Church to undergo, into these strippings it imposes on Him, into those negations it sets up against Him; but also into the riches it brings Him, into the growth which it gives, into the life which springs up unceasingly. Yes, the Church dies and lives in each period of her history. That is the reason why it is by entering as fully as possible into the very actuality of the life of the Church that the Christian attains the eternal.

It is because the whole Church is subject to the paschal rhythm that the Christian—in her and through her—is united with the Mystery of Christ. Each one of us dies to the world with her and lives in Christ in her. That is why we must grasp at each instant of history, that mysterious death of the Church in the world which follows that of Christ, and this new life which she finds again in Him. We must understand the Church in the paschal mystery in order to live of it with her.

7

THE CHURCH IN THE PASCHAL
MYSTERY

1. *The Church with respect to the movement
of history.*

With respect to all the great movements of history,
with respect to all human riches, it seems that the
Church's attitude is primarily one of refusal and of condemnation. It seems that she first turns aside, and then
turns her back upon the world which turns to her, which
ascends painfully toward her. It is only after many years
and sometimes centuries, that the Church accepts, welcomes, takes to herself the fruit long ripened in the sun of
history. Humanly speaking, one could call it a late recov-
ery, a refocussing of her decisions, and because of that,
a sort of delay, a setback, with regard to the movement
of history. The Church lives on the past instead of con-
structing the temporal future of the world. She always
comes along as it were after the fact to baptize a world
born without her. Some will see in that a sort of policy
of accommodation and submission to the *fait accompli.*

We must see in it something quite other. We must discover in that, in faith, a law of the transcendental action of the Church on history, the procedure of God's own action on humanity. Let us take an example. The Church condemns technical progress that affirms itself to be independent of transcendence. She condemns every materialistic and closed organization of the world, every undertaking of the salvation of man by man and of happiness without God. Since this world of work, historically closed to Christ, is the movement which is building the world, the Church seems to be opposed to the movement of history, she seems to stay aloof from what is being done in history. This sufficiency of work as the first value in the organization of the world is affirmed in Marxist thinking; the Church refuses Marxism as a conception of the salvation of man by the work of men.

The Church condemns this world, not only because it is opposed to her, but because it is opposed to man himself. The happiness it proposes is a mirage. She knows that. She condemns this technical civilization to the extent that it closes itself in on itself. She refuses the idea of man reduced to worker. She condemns it in order to make man realize his sin, and the facts that make her right are there. She condemns it in order to open man up to grace.

It is this opening up of the world of work to transcendence in grace and this taking in of all the riches of the building of the modern world, which is the task of the Church of today. Each one of us, in his place, must get into it. That is what is in preparation. That is what is already in the process of being done.

It is not in vain that these movements which are

slowly penetrating the modern world, the world of work and the world of thought, with a Christian spirit, have names of youth: working youth, farm youth, student youth.* A new generation of the Church is on the march. It is a beginning, a renovation of her action in the world.

2. *The life of the Church has its own rhythm.*

In order to grasp in a light of faith what constitutes the mystery of the Church in history, it is altogether insufficient to see her, as we have just done, face to face with the great building movements of humanity which she confronts one by one and penetrates. We have to go further and ultimately discover that through all of that, aided by all that, the Church herself lives, grows and is purified. Her history is not only ordered from the outside by the demands of her action and of her reactions on the world; she is ordered from within by the very rhythm of her own life, which is to complete in herself the mystery of Christ. The history of the world only assumes its complete meaning, in the Christian view, when one sees it providentially ordered to the fulfilment of the mystery of Christ in His Church. It is only in this perspective that everything around us falls into order and that we ourselves are ordered at once to the heart of the movements of history and to the center of the Church's life.

If indeed we look, with an all-encompassing glance, at the triple evolution that has been accomplished, with respect to the Bible, with respect to the Pope and with

---

* Translator's note: The author is referring to the movements of French Catholic Action: JOC, JEC, JAC, etc., which have some counterparts in the U.S.: YCW, YCS, etc.

respect to the action of the Church, we cannot help being seized by the profound unity which presides over this triple evolution. Whether we are dealing with the thought of the Church, with her chief or with her influence, there is an abandonment of a certain temporal dominance for a renewal of spiritual power. The Bible and the teaching of the Church leave, on a larger scale, their rational autonomy to the sciences and to philosophy, in order to discover, in a new purity, their own proper religious values. The Pope abandons a large part of his temporal power and leaves to all States complete political autonomy, in order to affirm his spiritual authority and to obtain an incomparable influence. Catholic Action, finally, leaves behind all temporal dominance of the Church in domains which do not belong to her properly, in order to develop an influence which is larger than ever.

At the heart of this evolution, one has the feeling of seizing upon an internal law of development which concerns the very life of the Church in the world. History is moving toward a purification of the Church. This purifying effort is the Church in search of herself. Her progress has its rhythm: there is a certain detachment for a certain renewal, a loss for a gain, death for a new life. For this is really what we have had to recognize in each of these domains. Everything seems finished, life gone, the elements scattered, submerged by the forces of the world and the power of sin; and yet all is reborn, under the pressure of the Spirit, for a new life. Is there a more startling testimony of the presence of the Spirit in the Church than this perpetual rebirth? It is a law of her life in the world, not just today, but always. Unceasingly, in each epoch of her history, she dies in order to live again. In that she resembles Christ. It is not enough to say that she resembles Him: she continues Him. It is the same mystery that is accomplished in her —the mystery of the Cross, the paschal mystery, the mystery of a humanity which dies to the mortal world in order to resurrect in an incorruptible world.

Providence gives us, throughout the history of God's people, a series of images and as it were approximations, of this ultimate movement of a world which is crumbling toward a new world. It gives us images and preparations of that Pasch at the end of history, when it will be necessary to leave everything in order to find everything. We must leave behind the Egyptian establishment in order to leave for the Promised Land. It is the exile, and we have to see that initial construction of the Holy City and of the Temple destroyed in order to give place to a religious restoration and to an interiorization of hopes and of worship. The Roman world is crumbling, and in its ruins, it seems that the Church is going to be buried, but it is for a new expansion in the barbarian world. Today, Christendom is falling into ruins, but a new and more catholic Church is arising.

3. The Church develops according to the Paschal rhythm.

Throughout all that, the Church is dying and being reborn. The Church is developing according to the Paschal rhythm. At each stage, she is more detached, more holy, and still she is more radiant and more catholic. But the very rhythm of the Church's life in history is only the expression and the affirmation in time of her most intimate reality and of her mystery beyond all the ages.

Here we are at the heart of her divine vocation. The Church is humanity on the march toward God, humanity opening itself up to grace, humanity dying in Christ in order to live with Him. At each instant, the Church is as if dying in the world. Crushed by forces infinitely more powerful, submerged by the floods of a surging humanity which are opposed to her, ruined, choked, annihilated, dethroned, unmasked, refuted, humiliated, reduced to nothing by force, by weapons, by reason, by money, by trickery, by work, by science, by all the elements of the world. Tomorrow it will be all over and tomorrow it starts up again. Tomorrow it is the same mystery: the Church is there, always dying, and always living, more than ever living. St. Paul felt in his flesh and in his heart this incessant passing from death to life, which is at the core of every apostolic vocation: "As deceivers and yet truthful, as unknown and yet well known, as dying and behold we live, as chastised but not killed, as sorrowful yet always rejoicing, as poor yet enriching many, as having nothing yet possessing all things." [1]

Such is the condition of the Apostle. Such is the mystery of the Church. The Church draws each Christian along in this passage through death to the finding of the true life. For, in the end, this is the mystery of man which is accomplished in Christ through His Church: he must die in order to live. He must renounce his limitations, in order to open himself up to the gift of God and become himself. If he pretends to be sufficient unto himself, he is dead, he is less than a man. If he agrees

---

[1] *Cor.* 6:9-10.

to be filled up, he goes beyond himself and lives in God. There is for him but one road to the true life, it is the Cross. And that is why, by means of her conditions in the world, the Church unceasingly leads humanity to share with her the death of Christ, in order to enter into His life.

4. *The Christian participates in the Paschal mystery by his insertion into the Church.*

Here is the focal point at which our most personal life joins the collective life of the Church and enters into the history of the world. Grace and the virtues are only given us to make us share more and more intimately in the mystery of Christ, in His passing from this world to His Father, in His Pasch. But, for us, this mystery of death and of life is not only a rhythm of personal life; it is shared in the Church. It is not independent of her history. In each epoch, at the most secret heart of the development of human history, the Church is called upon to effect a double task, opposition to all sufficiency, and assumption of all richness. In each period, she is called in a new way to confront the forces of the world and to be inserted therein, to suffer, under the dominion of evil, a renewed passion, and by her death itself, to transmit a life which comes neither from the will of man, nor from the powers of the flesh, but from God Himself.

Every Christian is called to live in the Church, in a way adapted to the moment of history in which he is, this detachment and this shining forth, this death and this life. By Baptism we are destined to enter into the mystery of Christ. We fulfill our personal vocation only by participating in the paschal mystery of the Church, as she is actually carrying it out in the world. That is what permits us, by giving us fully to the Church, by plunging us fully into her historic destiny, to rise above that obsession of absorption in the collective which just recently led a Simone Weil away from all adherence to the social.

It is right to recognize that every total giving of a person to a human group, reduced to its historical dimensions, is madness. Whether it be a political party, a social class, a national movement, man is not made solely to give himself to the life of the group, to undergo the impulses of its orders, and to sacrifice himself to the necessities of its progress. He has a personal destiny—a vocation. It is his primary duty to defend this vocation, and to dominate the group so as not to give himself to it except in accordance with the judgment of that spirit and the consent of that freedom which seeks its light beyond the pressure of the collective. Otherwise, man himself is savagely destroyed for the profit of the social monster. That is the proper form of barbarism and slavery in the modern world.

But it is not thus with our adherence to the Church. In this case, in this case alone, our most personal vocation is to live in the collective, for the collective itself is personal: it is Christ. Our vocation is to enter, through the Church, into the very life of the Son and in the drive of the Incarnate Word toward His Father. Through her, we enter into the intimacy of the Divine Persons. She is the only center, transcending every particular vocation, where persons are able to meet without being degraded. The Church is the only perfect form of community of persons, because she makes us enter into the intimacy of the Divine Persons, which is formed in love. That is why our *most personal* vocation is to be, or rather to be reborn, in the Church. We are ourselves and we know our name on the human plane only by our insertion into a human family, and by the bonds which that gives us with the whole of mankind, but in reality we are not fully ourselves and we do not know our own name as long as we are not reborn through Baptism into the family of the Church, which binds us all together to God Himself. Our most personal destiny springs up in her bosom and depends upon her. That is why she is really our mother.

By that very fact, the most intimate rhythm of our personal life is the rhythm itself of the Church's life, or rather of the life of Christ in her. To give our life over to the life of the group in the Church is not to submit a personal vocation to the deforming restraints of social pressure. It is to raise it back up to itself. Here it really lives the mystery of death and life for which it is made, here it discovers its real bonds with the universe, and the point of insertion of its own action into the world. It is in the Church and by participating in the life of the Church that it becomes itself. For not having made this fundamental discovery, the life of the Christian risks being misled. The growth of his personal holiness as well as the rectitude of his action are compromised.

On one hand, the purification of the soul can only be brought to its conclusion in the Church and through the action of the Church. The essential renunciations cannot be those which the soul chooses for itself. However great these renunciations might be, however heroic they may seem, they have the radical defect of having been chosen by itself. They still proceed from personal will. They could even be in the direction of the most secret tendencies that might have to be mortified. They may harbor I know not what personal satisfaction and what hidden pride in the determination we have concerning them. In a word, they are still impure, because they proceed from ourselves.

That is why all the saints have always recognized that the most profound purifications presupposed the entrance of the soul into a disposition of availability or of passivity with regard to the action of God. This action of God, which infinitely surpasses our concepts and our aims and which by that very fact disconcerts us, can arise in the inmost recesses of the spirit and well up from the depths of the soul. It happens in a more common and more constant way through the influence of the Church. Here too the Christian or the apostle must be available to the action of the other—they go into a receptive passivity. It is that which eliminates the roots of one's own will. We have to accept this view of faith, enter into this purifying design of God, in order to accept that the Church should try us, force us to the most costly renunciations, and literally, mortify us. In her and through her, we pass through death in order to enter into life. If he does not agree to enter into this perspective of purification by the Church, the Christian may perhaps impose on himself some difficult personal mortifications, yet he will pass right by the essential renunciations, which are the very ones that God requires and through which He destines us to enter into His providential action on the world.

5. *The Christian participates in the Paschal mystery by his involvement in the actual history of the Church.*

This entrance into the Mystery of Christ through submission to the exigencies of the Church, is not independent of her history. It is in response to the calls for Redemption of the present world that the Church solicits us to share in her mystery of death for life.

We indicated before the triple plane on which the Church actually is undergoing a sort of purification: the plane of thought, with the Biblical renewal, the plane of influence, with Catholic Action, the plane of insertion into the temporal, with the evolution of the position of the Papacy and the clergy in the modern world. We cannot remain strangers to this evolution. Each Christian is invited to unite himself with this internal movement of the Church which is the condition of her life and of her shining forth in the world. It takes courage to be realistic.

In our reading of the Bible, in our methods of influencing, in our temporal props, we must know how to strip ourselves in order to be renewed under the guidance of the Church. In all these fields, and in multiple ways, we must die once more to the world in order to live again in Jesus Christ. To refuse ourselves this is to refuse ourselves the most profound renunciations that the Spirit demands of us. But we must submit to these renunciations which are imposed upon our thought and our action, within the Church, that is to say, in the rhythm that the Spirit imposes on her history and according to the directives of those who maintain her in unity. There is no doubt that in this drive toward the future, there will be an almost fatal and perhaps necessary tension between those who have a greater share of concern for progress and those who cling to the good of tradition, those who have a greater measure of concern for adaptation, and those who have more of the sense of continuity. Their tension constitutes the life of the Church and assures her movement, and their submission to the same Hierarchy maintains her unity.

Nevertheless, we must keep ourselves from a too simple view which would abbreviate the plan of God by suppressing one of its essential dimensions. We must not idealize the real, but see what it is, in an outlook of faith. The concrete action of the Church in the world is not entirely pure, because it is not exclusively divine. It is also the action of Church men. The latter have not only their temperaments, but their faults. Our faith in the Church does not consist in denying this aspect, but in going beyond it. We do not state that the Church, in her decisions, is not subject to human influences, but we do affirm that she is subject to the influence of Christ. By faith we are assured that through these human influences, Christ leads His Church, purifies her, sanctifies her, conserves her, in order that, through an ever-more intimate detachment from what is evil in the world, and an ever-larger assumption of what is good, she is preparing in herself the Kingdom of Heaven. The human aspect of the Church's action brings on her some historical oscillations: the divine impulse confers upon her that unity which goes beyond history in order to make her enter into the eternal. Our faith in the Church is that God makes use of man to sanctify man. God makes use of the human to make something divine. There is His triumph, there is His glory. Therein is His plan, that the angels themselves contemplate in the Church and never cease admiring. That is why, in accepting the action of the Church on our lives, we are sure, at the very moment when the instruments God uses appear human—too human—to us, that she is guiding us, purifying us, sanctifying us.

For the apostle, this purifying influence of the Church's life concerns not only his personal life, but also his action. Actually, they are but one. He forms one flesh with his action, he is fulfilled in it. He can only be purified if his action is purified. That is why God pursues him on the level on which he engages himself totally. What we were saying about personal mortification is also valid, and perhaps even more valid, here. All apostolic action, however excellent, however generous, however detached it might be, needs to be purified. It proceeds normally and necessarily from the initiative of the apostolic man, based upon the needs of a definite milieu. Thereby it conceals an equivocation and a danger. For it is not the initiative of man that saves the world, nor is it the action of man that divinizes it. It is necessary that all danger of self-sufficiency be removed from apostolic action itself.

It is for this reason that every apostle is called to detachment from his action. His activity itself must enter upon a regime of passivity. It must pass through submission in order to remain a mission. It must accept a deep and profound renunciation of the germ of self-will, of the human plan that had been formed there, in order to enter purely into the design of God. It is the paschal mystery in the life of the postle. That is done in him through the Church. It is submission to the Church that effects this purification and mystery in us. It is by accept-

ing the directives of the Church regarding our action
that the latter ceases to be a personal plan to be carried
out by our own powers and becomes the design of God
confided to His grace. It ceases to be an undertaking and
becomes a mystery. It ceases to be a human adventure,
and becomes the mystery of Christ.

But that presupposes a painful journey, a death, a passion, a Cross; a journey all the more painful because for
the apostle, it involves not only his personal life, which
he would sacrifice a thousand times, but his action and
all those whom it attains, for whom he has given his soul.
A journey all the more painful because it implies not
only renunciation of all wealth, in poverty, the renunciation of all affections, in chastity, but the renunciation
of the spirit, in its very desire of salvation, in humility of
heart. A necessary passage, since it implies that we are
placing our plan of salvation in the hands of God. We
have the feeling of losing everything, and it is here that
we must gain everything. Here is the act of faith of the
apostle. As long as we have not accepted the salvation of
the world according to God's plan, at the price of sacri-
ficing all that is most dear to us, as long as we have not
chosen the Church in preference to all personal activities, we have not entered into the Passion of Christ and
we cannot have access to His Resurrection.

But to him who has given all, God gives all. It is
God Himself Who fulfills the desires of him who does
all His will. To the one who gives up to Him that which
is dearer to him than anything else, his very desire of salvation, God grants to save. The action we have given up
to Passion, through obedience, the life we have delivered
up to the Cross, through love, God will return in His
measure, and not only on behalf of the one who is dead,

but for a multitude of others. It is from the Cross that Redemption springs forth. It is the paschal mystery. It is through the Church and in her that the apostle shares in it and that his desire of saving, by dying to itself, is fulfilled in God.

8

THE MISSIONARY SPIRIT

IF WE LIVE in the Church, it is necessary that we be animated by her spirit. The Church is "on a mission" in
the world until the end of time. To unite ourselves with
her life is to enter into her mission, to be a missionary.
That is perhaps more demanding than we think.

It is a fact the importance of which we could scarcely
exaggerate: the missionary spirit has taken on, beneath
our very eyes, a new vitality and drive. Need we say that
this missionary drive, the opportuneness and authenticity
of which are indisputable, does not go forward without
posing some questions. First of all, a sort of infatuation
threatens to devaluate words and to end by taking the
savor out of the realities themselves. In a climate of pub-
licity such as ours, whenever a renovation is necessary,
everyone talks about it, everyone wants to be part of it.
The upshot is that no one knows just what it is all about.
When everybody wants to be a missionary, we end by
not knowing any more who really is a missionary. It is
necessary to define the meaning and the requirements of
the missionary vocation.

From another angle, the missionary life itself and the commitments it demands, pose problems. The missionary apostolate is not something done once for all. It is not just a state of life and a job obtained; it is a perpetual discovery of the Christian exigencies of a situation which is incessantly being renewed. The line of missionary penetration, through which it is at the advance point of the Church's effort, is subject to multiple pressures. Because it is fully engaged in a complex and moving reality, the missionary apostolate must constantly renew its decisions, specify its choices. Because it commits the Church, it must unceasingly verify whether this difficult effort which must adapt itself to the shape of events, is maintaining, in its general orientation, the correctness of the Spirit of Christ. No son of the Church can be uninterested in this effort in which we are all engaged. That is why we must all seek to understand better what the Spirit expects of us, He Who spreads forth in the Mystical Body of Christ the diversity of gifts and of functions while maintaining therein the unity of Charity.

1. *Christ, the ideal of the missionary.*

It is a fact that at every period of her history, the Church has been missionary. Her life is marked by a series of departures for the missions. Never can she rest on acquired positions; always we have to leave what we have, what has been won, in order to seek that which has not yet been reached, that which has not yet been touched. Each discovery of a new continent, each exploration that reveals new peoples, opens to her a new mission field. She runs to it: these peoples are made for her, she is made for them. It is an internal pressure that pushes her to meet all of mankind. Everywhere where there are men, the Church feels herself drawn; wherever there is something human, she has a mission to accomplish. Much more, this expansion is her life. She only preserves her institutions, her Sacraments, her doctrine, in order to give them to others, to bring them afar off. Her structure is missionary. She lives to missionize.

If we wish to find the source of this extraordinary power of expansion of the Church which is manifested in history, we must look into hearts. There are always in the Church, in every century, men and women, young men and young women, who have felt in themselves the desire to carry the knowledge of Christ, His Gospel and His grace, to people whom they scarcely know—a desire so powerful that it was necessary to leave family and country to go afar off, to live and die in the midst of an unknown people. This mysterious desire, more tenacious in the Christian heart than the call of gain in the merchant, more adventurous than the taste of discovery in the explorer, stronger than national ambition in war lords, is the missionary calling.

At the root of these callings, to explain them all and to account for their unity, their continuity, their expansion, there is the design of God Who loves all men and wishes to reach them all. Through this great missionary act of the Church in history, which pursues mankind throughout the entire earth in order to bring it back to unity, we rejoin the plan of God, the action of God and that effort of the Father Who comes to meet the prodigal, to reach out His arms to him and to bring him back to the paternal household. The wellspring of all missionary drive is the love of the Father for all men.

But that which commands every missionary effort is

the manner in which the Father chose to manifest His love to men: "God so loved the world that he gave his only-begotten Son." [1] The primary mission, and ultimately the only one, is the one which Christ receives from the Father, to communicate His life to men. The Father sends Him to men, because He so loves men as to give them His Son, but above all because He so loves His son as to give Him men.

What we must see and emphasize at the very outset is that this order of mission is an order of incarnation. In order to give the life of God to men, Christ takes on their life. To teach the thought of God and to pronounce the Word of God, He speaks their language. In order to communicate the Spirit to them, He is made flesh and dwells among us. It is the first mission. The Son of God leaving, so to speak, His state of glory, quitting the heavenly country, abandoning the assembly of the angels and all the eternal choirs, comes among men, becomes like unto them, save sin; more than that, He is one of them. By this very fact, He has introduced in humanity, into the web of human generations, into the human fabric, a new life which spreads unto the ends of the world. By being one of them, He has become a partner to their misery. He accepts its consequences, even to death and death on a Cross. By that very fact, by offering Himself for it, He atones for it and merits a new grace for all men. By being one of them, He has made them partners of His glory. Son of man, He has made them Sons of God. And the Good Shepherd returns to Heaven, to the angels and to the Father, burdened with that lost sheep, bearer of this sinful humanity for which He had left all things.

---

[1] *John* 3:16.

He thus presents to the Father a new humanity, a reprieved humanity, a reconciled humanity. Man, purified in Christ, has rejoined God. Christ is missionary by His Incarnation. But His mission is not completed with His passage on earth and His Incarnation is continued in the Church.

2. *The missionary vocation in the Church.*

Christ received the mission of saving all men. He received grace to communicate the divine life to all human families of all ages and of all countries. His love for men, His desire to reach them, is already universal and catholic in His Heart. Still, His Incarnation itself limits His presence to a definite epoch and His action to a definite country. This kind of antinomy in the mission of catholic Incarnation that Christ received from the Father, is resolved in the Church. The overflow of the love of Christ for men, that which He was unable to express in His human acts and in His earthly action, is poured out into the hearts of His apostles. As the Father sent Him into the world in order to show it His love, so Christ sends His Apostles to spread His charity. "As the Father has sent me, so also I send you." [2] The same Spirit of Love makes Christ present to this world, and raises up the Church in order to bring Christ to the ends of the world.

That is why we could hardly over-emphasize the fact that the Church is essentially missionary. She has received the same mission as Christ: to bring divine life to all mankind. That is the drive which upholds her efforts and organizes her structure, from the first day of her his-

---

[2] *John* 20:21.

tory until the last, from Pentecost to the Parousia. To say that she is catholic is to say at the same time that she is missionary. This catholicity *de jure* by which she possesses divine life in order to transform all human reality, this catholicity of structure by which she is organized in terms of the gathering of the whole of mankind around a single Leader, are but the principles which sustain that catholicity on the march which is her mission in the world, resulting in catholicity *de facto*, which will be her unfolding in heaven. The missions are catholicity being realized, the Church being formed, the Catholic Church becoming herself. The missions are the life of the Church.

But the Church performs this mission as Christ did, by means of an effort of incarnation. It is not from afar off that she saves people, it is by being part of them. In the same way that Christ takes on the perfect integrity of human nature, just as it is except sin, in order to lead it back to the Father, so too the Church, in each of her stages, must take into her unity the diversity of human families and nations, in order to lead them back to God. Divine grace respects the human nature which it fulfills, by communicating life to it. Thus the Church respects the civilizations and the races, the cultures and the peoples that she leads in herself to human unity.

This presupposes, at each stage of the Church's development, a missionary action which renews the action of the Incarnation itself. By an admirable disposition of His Providence, God has permitted, God has willed, that this effort of love which seems to be absolutely proper, absolutely reserved to Him, and which consists of giving Himself, of leaving the homeland to come to earth, God has willed that this act of love properly divine, should be imitated and shared by His Apostles. Every true mission participates in this effort of Incarnation. The true missionary leaves everything in order to give himself entirely to an unknown people and *to be of it,* in order to communicate to it the life of Christ. The true missionary leaves all, his family, his father, his homeland, his customs; he leaves his parish and the Church itself as an organized Christendom, and he leaves Jerusalem, to go to strange peoples who know not Christ and are not established into a church. He has lost the titles of nobility of his family, the refinements of civilization of his country, the whole environment of his origin, in order to enter into simplicity and impoverishment, and also into the goods and the enrichment of a new people, to whom he brings grace. He himself thus enters mysteriously into this *kenosis,* or abasement, of the Word of God, through which He left behind the splendor of His original glory in order to enter humanity through love for it, and in order to enrich it with His divine blessings, while receiving from it, with an admirable respectfulness, all human riches.

3. *Two forms of missionary vocation.*

And so it seems to us that we must distinguish in the Church two forms of missionary vocation. On one hand the whole Church is missionary. She is born of God, entirely formed by the Spirit in the bosom of the Father; her homeland is heaven. Her normal place is to be united with the choirs of Angels in order to praise God. She is already no longer of this world: "They are not of the world, even as I am not of the world." [3] Yet she lives in

---

[3] *John* 17, 14.

this world: "I do not pray that thou take them out of the world, but that thou keep them from evil." [4] Christ prayed that she might be preserved from evil, but not that she should be removed from life in the world. Not only is the Church subject to this law, but she accepts it, she consents to it from her heart—it is the Will of the Father. If she were not at that point by necessity, she would reach it by choice. She accepts to live in the midst of sinful humanity, to share its conditions of life, to be born incessantly in it, so as to spread in it the seed of the divine life. She unites herself with the world, she urges it to a conversion and to a choice, she passes judgment in proposing the divine blessings, but she receives all human riches, she assimilates everything that is to be saved in order to repatriate it in herself.

The Church is on mission until the end of the world. And every Christian must, in her, one day consent to this missionary condition. Every Christian receives divine life, every Christian already belongs to the City of God, but he agrees fully to live in the world and to be of it, as Christ was of suffering humanity, in order to love all men and bring about their return to God. Every Christian is charged with a mission, every Christian is charged with a part of humanity to conquer, which he has to cause to make its way to God, its exodus and its Pasch, its grand return to the Father. Every Christian is a missionary, born into the Church by Baptism, by uniting himself with the Incarnation of Christ in this world in order to return with Christ charged with a humanity redeemed in the mystery of His Passion, His resurrection and His glorious Ascension.

But if that is true, it is also true that, on the other

---

[4] *John* 17, 15.

hand, the missionary vocation remains a special calling in the Church. Certain persons are especially called to carry out in a visible way, through a particular state of life, the missionary spirit of the Church. They become incarnate in the concrete, they bring out in a forcible way, manifest in a striking way, the missionary law of the life of the Church. These are they who have left all, family, homeland and parish of origin, in order to introduce themselves, living, into a non-Christian milieu, so as to reap the human riches of this milieu, to unite them to Christ in His Church, in order to bring thereto, along with the gift of themselves, the life of Christ. They have given themselves to this environment, which is not that of their beginnings, and which is not as yet organized into a church, in order to bring it Christ. They have become incarnate in it in order to save it. They are missionaries in the full sense.

And so all are, in the Church, missionaries in the wide sense, because all agree to live in the world and to be in the Church, in order that she might bring to the whole of mankind the gift of God, in order that she might bring it back toward the Homeland. They participate in the general mission of the Church. But only certain ones are missionaries in the full sense because only certain ones are called to leave everything in order to give themselves completely to a people that was not God's people, to implant therein the Church and to join it with the humanity redeemed in Christ. By their whole life, these manifest to the world and to the Church herself the missionary orientation of her destiny.

It seems to us that this distinction is valid not only for the missionary vocation, but for every special vocation, which translates in this way, in the pure state and in a manifest fashion, the great invisible and hidden orientations of the Church's life.

We might say that the Spirit is thus pleased to show forth, in some, the riches of life that are common to all. In them, He makes us all recognize the call which, expressed in a striking way, secretly vibrates in their hearts and is part of their common vocation. In this way the different features of the face reveal the riches of the soul. In them, the Church recognizes, as if placed in the light of day and expressed in actions, the secrets of her mystery, the exigencies of her vocation.

Thus the whole Church is a virgin, that is to say, consecrated to God. She expects her fruitfulness not from the powers of this world, but from the virtue of the Spirit. In a real sense, all Christians participate in the virginity of the Church. They are all consecrated, they have renounced the world, in order to expect only from God their fulfilment, their joy, their eternal fruitfulness. It is to everyone that Saint Paul writes: "I betrothed you to one spouse, that I might present you a chaste virgin to Christ." [5] Nevertheless, there are those who have in a special way received the virginal vocation; they are called to manifest, by a particular state, this total consecration to God. They manifest in their flesh the requirements of transcendence with respect to every earthly affection and fruitfulness. They recall each Christian to the purity of his virginal vocation. They alone are virgins in the full sense. They alone have received a special vocation in order to show visibly in the world the virginity of the Church. Though the splendor which they show forth belongs to every Christian, it is to them that the Church awards the glory of virginity.

---

[5] *2 Cor.* 11:2.

In this way too the whole Church is priestly. She represents the whole of humanity before God. In her entirety, she brings the gifts of God to the world, she offers the world to God. All are priests in a certain manner, in the Church. It is to everyone that St. Peter writes: "You are a royal priesthood." [6] But some are called in a special way to manifest by their lives this total gift of self to God, in the name of others, this consecration to the things of God, which belongs to the whole Church. In them the priesthood of the Church appears to the eyes of all. To them alone the Church reserves the name of priests.

Finally, too, if we want to speak exactly, we must reserve the name of missionary to those who have received it as a special vocation and who have accepted its demands and its risks. He is truly a missionary who leaves the environment of his origin, in order to introduce himself sociologically and psychologically into a human milieu where the Church is not as yet organized, in order to implant the Church and to make Christ live there.

4. *Missionary vocation and contemplative life.*

Nevertheless, we must add that what counts principally before God is the gift of the heart. He who would live constrainedly in a milieu would be there in a much less real manner than he who has decided to leave it forever, but has been prevented from carrying out his plans. That is why the sick man or the contemplative may have an authentic missionary vocation in the total gift they make of themselves for an unknown people. There may be at this very moment missionaries in China or in Rus-

---

[6] 1 *Pet.* 2:9.

sia whose hearts have already crossed the frontiers, whose prayer and sufferings pour out onto an unknown land where the Church no longer speaks. The patroness of the Missions may have lived and died in a Carmel in France—yet her love embraced the earth.

It remains that this vocation always involves the secret wish and the effective will to share, according to the Will of God, in all the conditions of life of the milieu to which one consecrates himself. The departure may perhaps not take place, but it is really consented to. That is why even in the contemplative orders, with the encouragement of the Church, we see being born the desire to be inserted as much as possible and even to the intimacy of the method of prayer, in the life of the peoples to be evangelized. We know about the decisive push given to this contemplative form of the missionary life by Pere de Foucauld. His initiative forces us to set off more purely the very meaning of the missionary call . . . to carry out a Church-presence in a non-Christian environment, to take in all its riches by making them rise up in the Church to the praise of the Father. Must we add that this contemplative mission calls forth, as a necessary complement, the apostolic mission which announces the Gospel, brings the Sacraments and implants the Church?

And so, in the missionary effort regarding the pagan world, the entire Church must go forward. Contemplative and active, priests and laymen, the well and the sick, each must be at his post and linked with all the others. And this common effort in which the Church is formed and for which her functions are differentiated, completes and continues the effort of Christ Jesus coming into this sinful world to deliver it from its sin and to bring it back to the Father in the unity of the Spirit.

9

THE MISSIONARY CALL TODAY

THE CHURCH LASTS, develops, organizes, only in order to be missionary. She progressively becomes what she is: the Catholic Church. Her life is to bear testimony, to the very confines of humanity, to the love of the Father, the revelation and the communication of His life, through faith in Jesus. Her goal is to unite all mankind, with the unified diversity of its riches, in Christ, in order that with Him and in Him it might sing the praises of the Father.

We may say that the historical development of every form of civilization and of culture is providentially ordered to this introduction into the Church. It is there that everything ends and that every human form reaches its focal point and its fulfilment. Thus every form of human life and of social organization, every development of thought and every expression of beauty is a preparation for the coming of Christ. But at the same time, every human grouping is a call for the Church. It needs the Church in order to come to a conclusion. Its riches rot in egotistical foldings if they do not find the salt to

conserve them. Its unity becomes opposition or domination if it does not find a living focal point where it may
communicate with humanity. Its glory becomes idolatry,
if it is not enlightened with a light that turns it to God.
This call resounds in the Church. Without receiving any
message from the outside, she has rejoiced in the Spirit.
For the nations are destined to her and she needs them
to perfect the song of human praise of the Father's glory.
Each one of her members feels the flow of divine life
which demands in him this fulfilment of Christ. Every
human contact is a demand for the missionary spirit.

1. *Missionary expansion in the 19th century.*

The 19th century discovered the true dimensions of
the world. New methods permit the exploration of immense territories in Africa and the Far East. Means of
communication, the widening of international relationships, the world-wide repercussions of economic and
political problems, the international magnitude of social
movements, bring humanity to a progressive realization
of its unity. This large-scale contacting of new men, in a
humanity broadened to the dimensions of the world,
provokes in the Church a rapid and intense missionary
expansion. Numerous vocations, new congregations turn
toward new countries. The Church is founded, developed, organized, with native clergy and episcopate, while
at the same time the awareness of bonds of unity with
Rome is made more precise and is strengthened. The
Church grows simultaneously in extent, in diversity and
in unity; she lives. This growth is done at a pace so rapid,
in what concerns the implanting of the Church, that
there is a preview of the day when she will be established

over the whole surface of the earth, with a hierarchical structure based in the environments in which she lives. Persecutions themselves and hostility toward strangers accelerate the movement in this direction.

In a more or less proximate future, departure for a foreign country to bring the Gospel would no longer have any *raison d'être*, because each country would have recruited the messengers of the Gospel from among its own. Might not the era of properly-so-called missionary expansion soon be at an end? Might not the vocation of grand leave-taking, in which one leaves family and homeland to introduce, by the gift of oneself, the life of Christ into a new milieu, soon be without object?

2. New dimension of the missionary apostolate in the 20th century.

According to the ideas accepted up to now, we might have believed that. It would seem that, in the near future, the Gospel having been carried to the very ends of the world and the native clergy having been established in all latitudes, the period of missionary expansion would be at an end. The sign of catholicity, fully given, would only need to be fulfilled. But that would be to see the development of the Church primarily in her penetration of new territories, and, so to speak, on the surface. Now the 20th century is going to become aware of a new reality and explore a new dimension of the expansion of the Church. The Gospel having gone around the world, there remains to make it penetrate in depth. Not only are there many men not converted, enormous masses not evangelized, but human milieus which possess their own unity, their way of life, their culture, their riches, have not been reached by Christ. An overwhelming discovery.

We were so accustomed to a geographic subdivision of the missions, that instinctively, we looked for them far away, and were incapable of seeing the latter because they were too near. So taken were we with this habitual perspective that we believed initially that it involved only a problem of apostolate within the Church. We thought at first that an effort on the part of the clergy that was geographically in contact with these masses would suffice to discover in them the elements capable of renewing the Christian life in them, within the framework and structures of our parishes. It became necessary to recognize that this was an illusion. It became necessary to realize that there are social milieux which are foreign countries for the Church. She is not there. The milieux are as far from her as the people located at the antipodes. They will not accept that she should come from the outside, with the attitudes, the mores and the language of another milieu. One has to be of them in order to bring them Christ. One must therefore come out of one's own home, leave the house of one's father, abandon one's habits and one's environment, to become again a missionary.

The missions are no longer solely carried out at a distance, but close by also. Let us have no illusions about this: social distances are as difficult to negotiate as mileage distances. We may be as far away from a man who lives in the suburbs of our town as from a Negro in the middle of Africa. It is no longer geographic regions that one can situate on a map that have to be conquered for Christ, but sociological regions localed throughout the breadth of humanity. Thus, the reality of social classes, slowly forged by the economic development of the 19th century, long foreign to ecclesiastical circles, suddenly bursts into the Christian consciousness and shows the missionary problem in a new light.

A new world is living, growing, and suffering alongside us and we have to discover it—the working world. Three elements neatly pose the missionary problem in the working world.

First of all, it is really a new world. It was formed of a new social reality whose unity, which is manifested enough by common reactions, or whose originality and human riches, cannot be denied. "The human groupings around enterprises, the conditions of life, have given birth to new social relationships. In new sociological bonds, families of workers have formed communes of a particular nature." [1] Alongside some too-apparent deficiencies, the wealth of life of this milieu are great and extraordinary vitality though in conditions that are difficult, an undeniable community sense, a new sensibility and a development of human qualities of ability, of resistance, of courage, of thirst for justice, the aspiration toward a new world and a sense of human realities which surpasses national frames of reference.[2]

Yet, it is also a fact, actually, that these riches, made for Christ, are developed, abound and often are corrupted, far from the Church, and far from Christ. "Today, not only is there an enormous mass of workers that does not know the good news of the Gospel, but the working milieu, insofar as it is a world, does not show in

---

[1] Denis, *Monde ouvrier, terre nouvelle d'évangelisation,* in *Masses ouvrières,* 1951, p. 4.

[2] cf. P. Dillard, *Suprèmes témoignages.*

the Church a Christian community lived in the group-
ings of the popular milieu." [3]

Finally, not only is the working milieu aside from the
Church, it is psychologically far from her, turns its back
on her, does not see the path of its progress in that direction. It has been formed and given unity by a movement
of thought and action opposed to the Church and to all
religion: Marxist Communism. There is a frontier, more
than that, a sociological barrier, between the Christian
milieux and the working world. It is here that Catholic
Action results in missionary Action. It is undeniable that
worker Catholic Action has formed in the working world
militants who, despite their small number, by their living
and personal faith, are the authentic representatives of
the Church in the worker milieu. It is no less certain that
the presence of the action of these militants, far from
suppressing the missionary problem, poses it with more
precision.

As bit by bit they progress in their work, these militants, by the very fact that they are accustomed to the
methods of inquiry and to humble submission to facts,
measure its limitations in a better way. There is a con-
siderable portion of the worker milieu, especially in the
great cities, which is no longer touched by the action of
the Church and in whose bosom there is no more Christian presence. That is a fact. How will they be evangelized? How will the Word of Christ be addressed to
them? How, if there is no mission? In these sectors of
the worker milieu, there is no more leaven, nor salt; it is
necessary that Christians come there, live there, become
a part of them, in order to bring them the light of Christ

---

[3] cf. art. cit., p. 8.

and His life; in order to raise up there a new Christian
community adapted to the milieu, to implant the Church
therein. Missionaries are needed. The call is given not
only to priests, but to laymen.

3. Catholic dimensions of the missionary problem.

But we must not forget that if we have discovered
and felt painfully the dechristianization of the worker
world in France, the problem poses itself also elsewhere
in a way that is as grave and at times worse. There is also
a missionary call in the Church on a wider and wider
geographic plane. Who could forget those immense regions larger than the whole of Europe where Church
structures no longer exist? I am thinking of the immense
U.S.S.R. and the frontier zones. What Christian could
forget this innumerable people, those hundreds of millions of men, women and children who no longer know
Christ? What Catholic heart does not feel this absence
atrociously? Those peoples today lack a member to act
with, an organ to breathe and to speak with. It is a state
of violence to be thus separated from them. That cannot
last forever. Already we must be ready in heart and spirit
to bring them anew the life of the Church. For them
also missionaries are needed.

But is this mission not begun? Without any doubt it
is. For in the plan of God, so many lives offered in secret,
all the sufferings of exiled missionaries, all the atrocious
miseries of persecuted Christians, all the blood of martyrs shed at the frontiers of these regions where the faith
must be brought anew, are not only the seed of Christians, but the seed of missionaries and already for him
who believes, the certitude of the harvest.

Nonetheless, it seems that this determination of the sociological or geographical map of completely dechristianized zones, important though it may be, is perhaps not what is most profound in the present missionary call. It is in the depth of man that we must look for this unknown land where the Gospel has to be brought. It is not only in sufficiently large areas of its surface that the worker milieu appears dechristianized, it is in the deep folds of its mentality and in the very sources of the movements of thought and action which lead and unify it. It is not only in certain of its members, it is in its very soul. We have to reach here in order to open it to the message of Christ. It is not only a matter of individually converting a certain number of workers, it is a matter of giving to Christ the worker movement.

Whoever weighs the terms of this missionary requirement cannot fail to be frightened at what it represents. It is a new world which was formed in the face of the Church and more often against her—the world of technology and of work. It is not a case merely of drawing it to Christ, we must make in enter into the Church. That is not saying enough—we have to form the Church in it. It is necessary that it take on a Church form in Catholic bonds. It is not a matter of imposing on it a form of culture or of civilization. It is a matter of bringing it from the inside, in harmony with all the riches which are proper to it, faith in Christ and the community of charity with all Catholicity. That presupposes a conversion of the worker movement to the lights of Christian faith and hope, and an opening, a welcoming, an assimilation in the Church of all the values proper to the worker world and more widely yet, to the modern world. That does not presuppose a new Church, but a new phase of the life of the Church—not a worker Church, but the Catholic Church revealing a new aspect of her catholicity in the worker world.

The Church is not afraid of these problems; she is made for that. That is her missionary vocation. Our faith in the Church consists precisely in believing that she possesses in herself a transcendent source of life that renders her capable of receiving and assimilating while respecting them, all the historic forms of life and of human societies. She is missionary because she is divine. To believe in the divinity of the Church is to believe in her inexhaustible missionary possibilities, and to act according to this faith in the respecting of the structures of the Church and in receiving human values.

4. *Missionary progress and evangelical life.*

It would be vain to hide the difficulty of the work to be undertaken. Humanly, it is impossible. It would be completely wrong to consider the missionary work demanded of our times simply as an enterprise of men in which it is necessary to calculate the opposition and the forces. We would be lost. What is demanded of us is not primarily progress in action, but progress in faith. That is really the most profound meaning of the missionary call addressed to the 20th century. It is a call of God for a renewal of the faith of His Church in the grace of the Savior.

In what precisely does this progress of missionary faith consist? We must believe in the Church in a new way. In the face of these masses powerfully organized by technology, the Church seems again weak and immeasurably small. In the face of this world intent upon the organization of a human order in which happiness is assured by the resources of production, the Church seems inefficient, strange, and as though belonging to a world gone by. In the face of those who possess all the resources of this world, she has only the promises of God. We believe in the strength of God in the weakness of His Church. We believe that she brings to this world the only message that is able to save it from total ruin. We believe that beyond all her divisions, she forms a new world which alone will endure in Charity.

Such is the incomparable good, such is the salvation which she brings to the world. The community of Charity stored in the Church is at each epoch a transcendence of conflicts in which humanity loses itself. The most profound sense of her missionary expansion is to reveal a new dimension of her Charity in Christ. In an era dominated by the awakening of nationalities and marked by wars in which people come against one another, the Church owes it to herself to point out that her Charity is beyond all boundaries. Without tearing them away from their own countries, she unites men in a community which goes beyond countries. This meeting saves them. She is announcing the Kingdom of Heaven.

In an age of the world when the most profound conflict of mankind is the one which sets social classes in opposition, the Church is called on for a manifestation of Charity which surpasses all class spirit. That is divine. The effort of the missionary will therefore not be to be inserted into one class as against another, but to enter into a solidarity of life with a new social milieu, in order to call it to a community of charity which goes beyond all social categories and unites them in Christ. That is not easy. It is impossible without grace. Grace is needed so that the message of Charity may be borne. Grace is needed for it to be accepted. For there can be no entering into the Church without conversion. And neither are we able to bear the message of the Church without being converted unceasingly to the Spirit of Christ.

That is why we can hope for this meeting of Charity only in a divine surpassing . . . but a surpassing in the evangelical sense. That is to say, a passing by the narrow way toward the poverty of Christ. For such is, ultimately, the plan of God which conditions all missionary efforts. Such is the divine plan regarding history that St. Paul reveals to us in the Epistle to the Romans. That which is reborn in every age, that which divides humanity anew, is the eternal conflict of the pagan and the Pharisee. Through all the disdain of him who has, who sets himself up and judges, we must recognize the Jewish spirit being constantly reborn. Through all idolatry, all exclusive searching for a total happiness though the forces of man, we must recognize the pagan. Their opposition is constant, it is always tearing humanity apart. There is but one possibility of getting together, and that is to get together in Christ. But there is but one single avenue of access to Christ the Savior, and that is the awareness of sin.

Such then is the missionary attitude of St. Paul. He reveals to the pagan world its sin, its misery, its unconscious downfall. He reveals to the Jewish world its pride, its obduracy, its self-sufficiency. He encloses them in sin in order to open them to mercy. It is only as sinners, and in recognizing their sin, that they can meet before God. It is only as sinners that they have the same Savior, Jesus. It is only as saved by His grace that they find themselves again in Him. That is what we have to tell the world once again. We must announce the mercy of God spread forth by His grace, in Jesus Christ. We must announce salvation. For that, it is necessary that they all feel how much they need it. The Gospel must be preached to the poor.

Over and above the actual categories in which we express the missionary problem, over and above the worker world and the bourgeois world, over and above the East and the West, we must again enter into the evangelical categories or be lost. Nations cannot have access one to the other, classes cannot meet in peace, the wall cannot fall down, unless they come together before God in the humble awareness of their misery and of their sin, unless at last they know and recognize that they have all done evil and that they have done themselves wrong—unless they become aware of their poverty. There is but one country which goes beyond all the frontiers, it is that of evangelical poverty, that of poverty of heart: the Kingdom of Heaven. All may enter therein but no one, no matter from what country or what class he may be, can have access thereto except through conversion before God.

That is the true scope of the missionary call addressed to our time. Perhaps the immense void that the absence of these far-away peoples, the massive defection of a large portion of the worker world, created in the heart of the Church, is only the sign which permits her to feel more vividly now the great missionary problem of all the ages: the poor have not had the Gospel preached to them. There is an enormous mass of people who suffer and who struggle throughout the world in all countries and in all milieux, and whom Christ has not yet reached. Poor people are lacking in the Church. God thirsts for the poor—for these poor, these humble ones, these little ones who recall us to poverty before God. It is for them that the Church is made. If they were no longer at home among us, it would be a sign that we were no longer what we are supposed to be. They recall us to our mission. Their very absence is an appeal to the Gospel. The true missionary effort is to make oneself poor with Jesus Christ in order to welcome with Him all the poor among us.

10

EXIGENCIES OF THE MISSIONARY SPIRIT

THE MISSIONARY life is not an easy life. Like the vocation to virginity, the missionary vocation has some superhuman requirements that it is impossible to meet without grace; it is a supernatural vocation.

1. Missionary faith.

Every missionary vocation is first of all a call from God. God destines a particular member of His Church and leads him from within and from without, by an intimate desire, by events, and by the hierarchical mandate, to insertion into a non-Christian milieu, for the expansion of the Church in that milieu. This call demands an answer which engages all of life; spoken in the soul, it is translated into actions. This response is first of all a response of faith—Faith in the word of God and in His promises, for the formation of the elect people in an environment that is partially unknown. This faith presupposes, fundamentally, a confidence and a love for the milieu to which one is going, a confidence and a love of the Church with which one is marching.

That in turn presupposes that one has confidence in the possibilities and the riches of this human milieu. A natural and supernatural presentiment, a human and divine solidarity, make one believe that this milieu is capable of being opened to grace, of receiving the message, of loving Christ, of belonging to His Church, of becoming Son of God. In so doing, not only will it receive a grace of eternal salvation and even of expansion on the temporal plane, but it will bring into the Church new riches, to Christ a testimony of faith and love, a sincerity, a generosity, a homage which He has not yet received. It is respect, esteem, love, which sustain the missionary effort.

But it is also faith and confidence in the Church—a supernatural certitude that the grace of Christ is rich with a new and fully flourishing life which will complete them in their order, by making them sons of God; a certitude that the Church is capable of raising up in her bosom a veritable Christian community from among this people; a certitude that she towers far enough above all nations, all classes, all civilizations, to bring into her unity this nation, this class, this civilization, without denaturing it, without doing violence to it, but by fulfilling it and integrating it into Christ. It is, in a word, to believe in the catholicity of the Church and in the universality of Redemption.

We might perhaps say: missionary faith is believing in man, in this concrete milieu, and in his capacity for being divinized; it is believing in Christ in His Church, and in His capacity for giving a new life to this same environment. But it is rather believing in God, believing that the entire work of God the Creator is good and ordained to be accomplished in the work of Christ the Redeemer, through His Church.

2. An effort of Incarnation.

This faith is translated into an effort which engages the entire life of the missionary and fulfills his vocation. Missionary effort is primarily a departure. We are familiar with the solemnity of those departures in missionary institutes. But it is not enough to embark, in order to leave. It is not enough to leave materially a house, a country, a family—those things are difficult, but still relatively simple. It is a matter of stripping oneself of a multitude of habits, of ready-made judgments, of reactions, of feeling, of human conveniences, in a word, of a whole mentality, in order to be introduced into a new milieu. It is a matter of leaving behind the way of life of one's environment of origin not only geographically, but psychologically. This stripping has a positive aspect, which is the principal one—it is an insertion, an incarnation, into the new environment. The missionary is not making an excursion, a trip, undergoing a phase, an experience; he enters this milieu without any idea of returning. He is not coming to talk to it, he is coming to live there. He is not coming to study it, he is coming to *be of it*—it is a new life. A man leaves behind a certain way of life in order to take on a new one. More precisely, it is by making himself part of this new milieu that one is called upon to strip himself of the old habits.

Thus Christ—it is by becoming incarnate that He strips away the splendor of His divinity. Every mission-

ary takes up this gesture in his own way. He becomes
incarnate in a milieu. This insertion is not an act of con-
descension, it is an act of love. One does not bend toward a milieu, one is part of it. We should write: one is
born of it. That is what the Word of God did. He does
not lend Himself to humanity; it is the latter that gives
Him a new birth. He is the one that allows Himself to
be formed, lets Himself be taught, in order to be man.
During His whole mortal life, the Epistle to the Hebrews
tells us, "He . . . learned obedience from the things that
he suffered," [1] He received the lesson of humanity, He
let Himself be taught the human condition. Thus the
missionary receives from the milieu in which he participates, as it were a new birth and a new being, an increase of humanity. It is impossible to describe the
gestation of this missionary formation. It is the slow
work of the conditions of living, of dwelling, of work, of
the nature of food, of settlement, of distraction, but also
of common difficulties, of everything that establishes the
solidarity of life. To seek to escape that is to lack the
missionary spirit. To be available, humble, receptive, in
order to let oneself be fashioned, body and soul, to be
one of those in whose midst we live, is to become a
missionary. That presupposes a stripping away, a renunciation, the notion and force of which only the actions
of the incarnate Christ are able to give us.

On the other hand that does not mean that the attitude of the missionary has to be purely passive. Far from
it, it is astonishingly active. First of all, in penetrating
into a new milieu, it enters into its life. A new tongue,
new preoccupations, new aspirations, leisure and culture,

---

[1] *Hebr.* 5:8.

work and solidarity . . . he enters into everything that makes up the life of this environment. But he enters it as a Christian; that is essential to his mission. Before God, he has to make this milieu agreeable to Him, by offering Him all that it has of human riches, in a filial gesture. He cannot offer what might be sinful. Before men, he has to bear the witness of a life completely similar to theirs, but fully Christian, fully according to Christ, fully evangelical. The very meaning of his missionary life is to show in his life that this can be—that one can be part of that concrete humanity as a son of God. To abandon one of these two goals, respect for the concretely human or respect for the divine, is to fail in one's mission.

That is why the Epistle to the Hebrews tells us that Christ, coming into this world, became in all things a man like other men, save sin, *absque peccato*. That presupposes on the part of the missionary a constant, extremely difficult effort.

3. *Missionary detachment.*

An attempt to clarify: the missionary can and must leave aside many reactions acquired in his environment of origin, reactions which make him belong to a category of men different from the milieu of the mission; *a fortiori* if they were not only too particularized, but also opposed to the evangelical spirit. But he cannot leave behind what is the Christian spirit itself, the Christian reaction, the Church attitude, because it is precisely the reaction of the Church which he is to bring and to adapt to the milieu in which he finds himself. There is therefore a profound discernment to be made in order to uncover what might come from man and from one's belonging to a particular milieu, and what comes from God and from the very exigencies of the filial spirit. The missionary must not bring into this milieu the way of doing things and of reacting of another environment, the domination of another mentality. He is not charged with colonizing, but is to bring the purity of the evangelical spirit.

This of course demands a judgment of prudence that has nothing about it of a mathematical equation or of a chemical analysis. For in every civilization, in every culture, in every particular mentality, there are universal elements which can be addressed to men of all nations and of all classes. Moreover, there are contacts between diverse cultures which are beneficent for all and of which the missionary can be the instrument. He remembers enough of his milieu of origin to make it known and loved by others. It remains that his proper mission is to bring the Gospel, the life of grace, and not a particular form of civilization or a particular mentality. That imposes on him a discernment in what he brings: a return to evangelical purity.

But on the other hand, discernment is required in what he adopts. He must enter totally into the whole life of the mission environment. He must be part of it. There is no attenuation in that. But, if he has to participate in everything that constitutes the life of this human milieu, he must not enter into that which constitutes its sin. Here we find that fundamental confidence, in the missionary effort, in the basic goodness of every work of God. That presupposes in effect that this milieu is not radically evil, that one can truly enter into its life without participating in sin, that its life is not its sin, but requires, in order to be fully itself, only to be straightened out and to expand according to the lines of force of the Gospel.

There is a crisis here, the gravity of which we must not conceal. Missionaries have always felt how delicate it was to appreciate exactly in the actions or in the mentality of a milieu, what is truly incapable of assimilation by the Christian spirit. There too a discernment has to be made between what is custom, particular culture, or legitimate aspiration on the part of the milieu, and what might be idolatry, closing off, cult of the milieu itself, or depraving of morals. We call to mind the controversy which lasted centuries over the evaluation of the worth of acts of worship offered to one's ancestors, in China. Was this an idolatrous cult to be proscribed, or simply a family custom to be accepted and to be animated with the Christian spirit?

Likewise, in other environments, many elements remain difficult to evaluate. If it is a matter of pleasures, distractions, where is the exact borderline between what is simply not in accord with the conventions of a different milieu and what is truly opposed to the very delicacy of purity or of evangelical charity? It is only at the price of a great sincerity, of an effective control of the missionary community, with the help and counsel of the Spirit and in submission to the directives of the Church, after experience and perhaps mistakes, that this discernment will operate.

But whatever may be its importance, the question of pleasures is relatively secondary. One can remain aloof from some of its pleasures without abandoning a milieu. One cannot remain apart from what constitutes its collective aspirations without quitting it psychologically. Herein is perhaps the most delicate question that is actually asked of the missionary conscience. What to do if this movement, whether it be aspiration for national independence or for social justice, is mingled in fact with atheistic ideologies or with non-Christian sentiments?

It is certain that the solidarity of the missionary with the milieu of which he is a part must lead him to feel with it the injustices of which it is the victim, and to promote effectively a more just order which would satisfy the legitimate aspirations of this environment. If it is necessary to fight for that, how would he not be involved with that struggle? Yet, even if he has to fight along with the others, he must not fight like the others insofar as they are still pagan.

First of all, the missionary intention is difficult. The missionary cannot forget that he is there in order to bring a new spirit—the Spirit of Christ; a new dimension to human aspirations, the way open to the Kingdom of Heaven. If he got to the point of consecrating his life, his energies and his time exclusively or principally to the struggle for a temporal order, for the liberation of a people or the liberation of a class, he would become a leader or a militant, he would lose the missionary orientation. From the moment that the center of interest of a life, the essential fiber of the soul, the directing line of action, the passion which unifies the personality, places itself at the level of a human realization, of a new historic order, of the promotion of a class or of a people, the missionary spirit is in danger. That is its gravest temptation. It down-grades the essential. The authority of the Church will never be able to give a mission for the construction of a temporal order only. It is not on this plane that she is engaged.

The sin of the world is its self-sufficiency, its ceaseless aim for the salvation of man by man. If a man hopes for the salvation of a people or of a class by the intervention of a revolution, or of a man, he enters into its sin. If one enters into the exclusive solidarity of a group which refuses to open itself up to salvation by Christ, one is outside the Christian order.

It is a seductive temptation, because this mentality is common and seems to identify itself with the awareness that the milieu itself assumes; an attractive attitude, because it introduces us into the movement of the world which is making history, according to human appearances. It is here that missionary faith takes its position. The missionary does not expect salvation from a human order, from an economic or social revolution, but from the divine order which God establishes in the Church.

The supernatural effort of the missionary, upon entering into this group solidarity, will be to go beyond it; by taking it on and going beyond it, to help the others to go beyond themselves, for a catholic coming-together and a salvation that is Redemption. This conviction that the only true salvation comes from Christ animates the life of the missionary. It is this salvation which he brings.

Thus the missionary in a working milieu must maintain two orientations which seem contradictory. He has to keep his solidarity with the worker's world, and in order to keep it, he has to work and struggle with it for the order of justice. He must transcend this aspiration for social justice in order to open the milieu itself to religious justice such as St. Paul announces it, which comes from the grace of Christ. But is this not the very paradox of every Christian life, which must work in this world for a temporal order while affirming that its ful-

filment will only take place by God's gift, in eternity?
The attitude of the Christian always involves attachment
and detachment, life in the world and transcending the
world. If he should let go of one or the other, he is no
longer according to Christ.

There will be as it were two forms of missionary vocation. One insists more on insertion, the other on transcendence; one on working with the world without rejecting the necessary renunciations, the other on renunciation without refusing the necessary action. It is
the vocation of the layman to be especially involved in
the construction of the temporal order so as to open it
to grace, and the vocation of the priest to be especially
detached from temporal tasks in order to consecrate
himself entirely to the building of the supra-temporal
City which re-unites all men in the Church. We may
conceive of a missionary life that enters more actively in
what is actually the promotion of the worker's cause,
being careful to disengage it from materialism, to raise
it above hatred and to open it to the only promotion
which saves man, which is the grace of Christ. But a
man may also be a missionary by accepting the worker's
condition, by sharing his lot and his aspirations, while
consecrating them to God and opening them to His
Grace in a more contemplative, more adoring, or more
apostolic form of life which seeks social action less than
it does evangelical radiance.

There is room here for the action of the layman and
for that of the priest, for that of the apostle and that of
the contemplative. One of the essential renunciations of
the priesthood, which consists in giving one's life, is in
this case to give one's life not directly for the promotion
of a temporal order, but of the Kingdom of God. It re-

mains that, in whatever form it may be, the life of the missionary is strangely difficult and rests entirely on Faith.

4. A vocation that makes martyrs.

What is the most painful for the missionary is that, in this heroic faith, he risks being misunderstood and attacked from all sides. If he were not galling to his environment of origin and to the environment in which he is living, then one would have to fear for him—he would be lacking something. The love of Christ for the Kingdom of Heaven, beyond all political liberation and all human domination, the love of Christ for all men, was so scandalous in the eyes of the Jews that they rejected Christ and crucified Him. It would not be astonishing if the missionary should someday run up against the same incomprehension, and by that which transcends men in what he brings, should shock them. He is therefore faced with a definitive choice: either to deny the transcendence of love and enter purely and simply into a human plan of combat, or to affirm his message unto death, and become a martyr. The missionary vocation carries in itself the germ of martyrdom. The universal love of men, the divine love of man, leads to the Cross . . . but through that painful passage wherein everything fails, everything ends. The sacrifice of Christ saves mankind and the missionary offering founds the Church. Christ Himself announces this failure and this success: "If they have persecuted me, they will persecute you also. If they have kept my word, they will keep yours also. Take courage, I have overcome the world." [2]

---

[2] John 15:20; 16:33.

The missionary effort which begins by uniting itself with the act of Incarnation of Christ, is fulfilled by uniting itself with His Sacrifice of Redemption and with His paschal mystery. The missionary who has entered with his whole being into a human milieu, into its struggles and its aspirations, carries it with him into his death and makes it enter with him into Heaven. He saves it. It is faith in the redemptive value of sacrifice which makes the missionary drive, through death, result in the salvation of those he loves.

5. Missionary disinterestedness and the sense of Church.

To say that the missionary life ends there is not to go to the end of its mystery. For just as the mission of Christ is not finished with Easter or the Ascension, but with Pentecost and the founding of the Church, so too missionary effort is fulfilled in the formation of the Church in the milieu in which it has made. The goal of its mission is to implant the Church. That presupposes, on the part of the missionary, a special detachment. He tends to raise up, in the milieu in which he lives, the community of believers which is the Church—a community whose life is Charity. This community of Charity must normally express itself in prayer and in worship, must be progressively nourished by the Sacraments, united in the Mass. This new Church, this portion of the Church, must tend to adult age, that is to say, it must tend to obtain for itself all the organs of its life: its clergy, its Hierarchy. It is a vital development, both normal and necessary. There is no fully constituted Church without it. That poses a multitude of problems. It implies the constant concern of the missionary for directing and encouraging this development, but also the courage to withdraw, if necessary, before the new elements of this indigenous Church, his mission having been accomplished.

There will therefore truly be a Church, the incorporation of this milieu into the Church. The life of this milieu, its soul, its art, will enter into the Church and will find their place there, in the Catholic stream. That obviously presupposes that during all the time of its development, this Christian community remained linked with the whole of the Church. There again the missionary effort is strained between contact with the periphery and bond with the center. This two-fold contact insures its mission. If it should lose contact with the milieu to be evangelized, there would no longer be a mission; if it should lose contact with the center, it would form a sect, not the Church. This contact with the center demands an order and a two-way conversation. The mission remains linked with the Hierarchy and the missionary mandate assures its integration into catholicity. But this essential juridical bond must be a bearer of life. There must be a two-way conversation. Let the missionary be able to speak in the Church and express the needs of his apostolate, in order to open the Church up to the appeals which come from the periphery and arouse the necessary reactions! But the missionary must also be able to listen. The facts he adduces are likely to inform the judgment of the leaders. The authority which the latter possess from Christ renders them capable of giving orders. Information from facts is a source of light, but the action of the Spirit in the Church penetrates and judges it. Submission to the orders of the Hierarchy is the real sign of faith in the action of the Spirit in the Church. Without this faith there is no more unity, there is no more Church.

6. *The whole Church in a missionary status.*

If this is to be the attitude of the missionaries regarding the Church, we may understand that the Church has some grave duties with regard to them. She is entirely missionary. She is completely interested in the missionary task. The fact that missionary action in a worker's milieu is brought to bear on the same geographic territory as that of the established Church and is inserted into her structures poses some new problems. Now it is the whole Church, as we perceive quite well and our Bishops have declared time and time again, that is engaged in the missionary movement.

That does not mean that the whole Church must adopt the methods proper to those who are missionaries in the full sense of the word. Especially does it not mean that every form of life, of prayer or of action other than those which belong to the mission Church, must be depreciated or considered *passé*. Distinctions must involve no separation, no distrust, no disdain. It is good that they should be respected. Under the pretext that the whole Church is missionary, it would be an error to want to suppress all the forms of life, all the structures of action of a Church which has its history and its traditions; it would be as false as to want the whole Church, which is virginal and adoring, to adopt in all her members the monastic way of life. There is a confusion between the missionary spirit which must animate the entire Church and the missionary methods which are the product of certain people, that would be greatly damaging.

It remains that the whole Church, finding herself actually in contact with those whom the Hierarchy directs to the worker's mission, needs a new understanding of what missionary effort is. She has to admit precisely that the missionary, in submission to the Bishops, has to employ procedures that are not to be considered as general rules, applicable to the entire Church. It is necessary to remain in close touch with the missionaries, by a fraternal love in Christ, by as wide an understanding as possible of their difficulties, more, by a common experience of the sufferings and the miseries of these people who are to be brought closer to Christ. This understanding, this common experiencing of the difficulties of evangelizing the world of work, this same suffering, this same effort, this same giving, these same trials will bring it about that we will be less tempted to judge one another severely.

But an open-minded and understanding attitude is altogether inadequate. The missions in the Church demand from us a concurrence active in other ways. The fact that they are in the same territory as a Church of parochial form involves new exigencies: opening up to missionary problems, understanding those who adopt new forms of Christian life by accepting that they be themselves, that they be different while remaining Christians and fully part of the Church; evolution from within toward forms of parish life which do not eliminate all the habits and customs of the milieu, but at least all that is opposed to the Gospel; flight from all guilty compromises with the monetary forces that would render it odious to the worker's world; all that is not easy, but has become absolutely necessary in order that one day, the missionary Christian community may recognize, in parish life, the Church and the very life of Christ.

That is indispensable, if the unity of the Church is to be maintained and so that two Christian communities which could no longer understand one another, should not be formed. It is one of the most urgent witnesses of the Church in the modern world to show the possibility of a human community which goes beyond the limits and antagonisms of nations and of classes. That does not presuppose, either at the start or at the end, a fusion of all things which would result in an undifferentiated mass. It does presuppose that, recognizing and accepting one another as different, we might recognize ourselves as sons of the same Father, in Christ and His Church. That demands on both sides enough fidelity to the evangelical spirit to live as sons of God and to recognize all others as brothers. This impetus of Charity which must work in all human areas and bring them to transcend their group solidarity in order to enter into a catholic solidarity, is the necessary condition if missionary effort is to result in the unity of the Church. Under pain of failing in our most urgent tasks, the world and God are pressing us to let pass through us a burst of catholic Charity.

7. *Spirit of Charity.*

For, ultimately, we have to come around to the great intuition of Saint Paul in the first Epistle to the Corinthians. Yes, in the Church there are a diversity of charisms, a diversity of gifts, a diversity of functions. We must consent to that. We must rejoice in that. It is this very diversity which makes the unity of the Church and allows her to act in the world. Our differences do not separate us, they render us complementary. This diversity does not set us in opposition one to another, it unites us in the same living organism. But beyond all diversities, beyond all gifts, which are distributed to each as God wills, beyond all the functions which are distinguished and hierarchized, there is Charity, which is common to all. There are some who have brilliant gifts, an admirable intelligence, an astonishing power of action, an heroic devotion. All that would be nothing without Charity. Charity is humble, mild and patient. It does not make itself noticeable. It is child-like. It loves everyone. It is helpful. It is good. It goes beyond all differences of race, of class, of nation. It surpasses all differentiations. It agrees to everything good which is done in the world. It contains all forms of commitment. It loves the poor. It loves all those who are in Christ. It loves those who are not yet there. It always expects something good from him who is the farthest away, the most scorned, the most hated, the most hardened. It is universal. It is catholic. It makes unity. It makes the Church. Without it, no matter what I may do, I am nothing. Without it, no matter what I undertake, I am wasting my time and scattering my energies. With it, however small and poor I may be, I am receiving the very life of God and I join, in the midst of my soul, all my brethren united in Christ.

11

CONTEMPLATIONS

IN A RECENT study [1] Fr. Plé was clearing the way to what he calls a "mystique of mysteries." Perhaps we could call it also a Church mystique. Can a man pray just as well, be united just as closely to God, receive just as fully the graces of contemplation, in acts of community life and action, in the reception or administration of the Sacraments, as in the calm of solitary prayer?

Put this way the question may seem strange. There is practically no one who does not admit in theory that one is able to pray just as well in the acts of the liturgical life and to contemplate within the framework of the Holy Mysteries, as in the silence of a completely personal prayer. But on the practical level, it is otherwise. When we speak of contemplation, we see as if by instinct a man immobile, silent, recollected. When we speak of the contemplative life, we think of the nuns and the monks who, within the walls of the cloister, sheltered

---

[1] Rev. Plé, *Pour une mystique des mystères,* in *Supplément de la Vie Spirituelle,* November 15, 1952.

from the agitation of the world and the preoccupations of action, plunge into adoration and praise.

Could it be true that the contemplative life can be the portion as well of those who, in the Church, in different ways, are through their ministry, as St. Paul says, the "dispensers of the mysteries of God"? Could it be true that the administration and reception of the Sacraments, and apostolic action itself, can become in the Church the riches of contemplation? This does not involve simply a practical question of knowing at what moment to pray—for we must always pray and never grow weary. It is a matter of the very nature of Christian contemplation, of knowing whether it is the flight of a soul which detaches itself from everything sensible in order to move toward a meeting with God, or rather the attitude of a purified soul which discovers and welcomes in the life of the Church and in its own action, the design of God for the world and for itself.

As the study which we have mentioned brought out so well, we must disabuse ourselves, from the very beginning, of a certain platonic concept of prayer that has penetrated even deeper than we realize into our Christian mentality. Prayer, in this view, would be an elevation of the soul to God at the price of detachment from the sensible. That which keeps us in the region of the shadow and of death, is the weight of the body and the opacity of things. We must tear ourselves away from all that in order to enter into the spiritual life and into the world of eternal realities. The ideal seems to be, ultimately, that of the separated soul which, detached from every link with earth, flies without fear toward the Good of God which draws it on.

Such a philosophy of prayer is basically at the bottom

of many of our reactions. No doubt, it is never presented in the pure state. No doubt lived prayer often rectifies errors regarding thought-about prayer. It remains that it is not useless to show how these platonic orientations would drive prayer into ways that are not those of Christian prayer. First of all, and this is a fundamental point, contemplation would appear as a sort of abstraction, of detachment from the sensible. Such is not the sense of Christian contemplation. The Platonian contemplates ideas. The Christian contemplates Mysteries. That is entirely different. The Christian mystery is caught up in the sensible. It is not a transcending of the world so as to by-pass it, but a supernatural understanding of the world in order to read in it the plan of God. The Christian does not seek spiritual realities outside of this world; he seeks the presence of God in this world. By that very fact, the indispensable detachment for having access to the light of God is not so much detachment from the sensible as from sin.

It is not so much a case of externally leaving behind every bond with the outside world, and of suppressing as much as possible all corporal activity considered as a weight on the soul. It is a matter of interiorly abandoning all links with the sinful world, and of suppressing as much as possible all corporal or spiritual activity marked by egotism and sin. The real weight that keeps us far from God is not the body, but sin. True recollection is purity of heart. This is an important distinction that marks the true direction of effort. It is not so much a matter of getting rid of the sensible and of one's links with the external world—an impossible and perhaps useless undertaking—but of living with the bonds in the fulness of Charity and of enlightening them with a light of

Faith. We must not quit our situation in the world in order to contemplate, we must live it fully as a Christian, that is to say, in the Church.

A second difference seems almost as important. Platonic contemplation remains an effort of man, a sort of surpassing of the ordinary conditions of life of which only the philosopher is capable. It is reserved to the power of the human spirit and is found at the end of its efforts. Christian contemplation is a gift of God. It is reserved to the humble of heart to whom God reveals Himself. It is a light of Faith which lights up the most modest of events in order to discern in them the action of the God of love and the fulfilment of His design.

That is why platonic contemplation is easily discouraging. The most powerful spirits find themselves soon wearied, exhausted, breathless, in the world of pure ideas. Begun in the optimism of confidence in the human intelligence which conquers immortality, it ends in a discouraged pessimism. The life of the gods is inaccessible to men. Christian contemplation begins and ends in Hope. It awaits, it calls, it tastes the gifts of God. That is why it is never confounded. The most humble realities nourish it; it finds in them a hidden manna: action, light, the very Presence of the One it is searching for and Who comes to it. The Platonian elevates himself to God in order to grasp Him, and misses Him; the Christian opens himself up to God in order to be seized by Him, and God does not fail him. How many discouragements in prayer come perhaps from the fact that we have sought in it the direction of an impossible abstraction from concrete life, whereas it is the divine meaning that God gives it when one discovers His presence therein. For that is the ultimate opposition. Platonic contemplation is a transcending of time, of the concrete conditions of life, of history and of the social environment. In detaching ourselves from the body we separate ourselves from the world, from others, and from ourselves, in order to enter alone close to God Alone.

The Christian life, even to its highest summits, leaves us one with all those who live in Christ. It is communitarian. It is the Church. Here the soul does not enter into a non-temporal world but is placed in the world of eternal life. It is altogether different. It does not abandon its time, it does not abandon its brethren, it does not abandon Christ and the Church, but enters into that center wherein time rejoins the Eternal in carrying out the plan of God, in which men rediscover unity by becoming re-united in Christ, in which the Church joins her Spouse by delivering herself to Christ, in which Christ joins the Father by giving Himself to Him in the Spirit of Love. It is life itself, the concrete life, the community life, life in the Church which, lived in faith and in love, reveals its mystery and discovers transparently the riches of God which animate it. It is the mysteries of God, fulfilled in our lives, dispensed by the Church, manifested through the Liturgy, that become the heart, the food and the support of contemplation. It does not abandon history, it enters into the event and grasps from within the direction of its effort toward the eternal accomplishments. It does not leave time, it penetrates it. It is prophetic.

In order to see God one must be dead to the world. And that is what the wall and the monastic life never cease teaching us with an irreplaceable eloquence. But, more than that, we must be living in the Church. And that is why all those who have renounced from their hearts, the sinful world, and live in Charity in the Church of Christ, are able to enter into possession of the inexhaustible riches which she discovers daily in her life, in her action, in her Mysteries.

1. *Contemplation is life in the Church.*

Our prayer is not a sort of effort of abstraction by which the soul transcends everything sensible and raises itself to the level of spiritual realities. It is at the same time more human and more divine—it is Christian; more human—our prayer does not separate us from everything sensible and from all men . . . we go to God just as we are, bound to the world in which we are born and to men whose brethren we are; more divine—it is not a matter of raising ourselves to God's level, but of welcoming Him coming to us. We must consent to the plan of God for the world and for us. We must discover Him, and therefore, read in the events of history, with the eyes of faith, the marvels He performs for us. We must discover the gift of God close by and let ourselves be taken up by it. That is why our contemplation attaches itself to Christ Jesus and to His Mysteries, in which God gives Himself to us. That is why it attaches itself to the Church in which Christ comes to us, and whose actions reveal to us His presence and communicate to us His life. We come into contact with God through Christ in the Church. Our contemplation is life in the Church.

St. Teresa has indicated strongly how the contemplative life remains, even in its highest peaks, bound up with the mystery of Christ. It attaches itself to Jesus Christ, it does not abandon Him, and in Him it finds God. In this it goes beyond all forms of religious contemplation, or rather it brings to a climax in itself, the desire that is common to them: to find God.

For the saint remains a man. He finds the spiritual only through the sensible. He cannot go beyond himself so as to place himself at God's level—an impossible undertaking of natural mystiques, which leads to despair. But God, by love, can place Himself within man's reach and give Himself to him; God gives Himself to us in Jesus. It is in Him that we discover God and constrain Him. He is the Temple in which God reveals Himself and the Spouse in which He gives Himself. There is no contemplation that goes beyond Him. He is the way and the goal. We must go through Him and enter into His mystery of death and life, participate in His Passion and His Resurrection, in order to have access to the Mystery of God. We must discover Him in order to know openly the Face of God; to grasp, through the mysteries of His human life, His divine Person, in whom we have access to the Father by the Spirit. We must let ourselves be enlightened by His light, penetrated by His love, vivified by His life; He is for us the way, the truth and the life.

But what is true of Christ we must also say of His Church. It is all of a piece. Christ lives in His Church. Participation in the mysteries of Christ is, for us, accomplished by participation in the life of His Church. The Liturgy is this sacramental bond which links the entire life of Christians and through them, all of mankind, with the mysteries of Christ continued in His Church. That is why, just as contemplation does not go past Christ to find God, so too it does not by-pass the Church but rather sets itself up in her in order to discover there, by transparence, God Himself Who gives Himself in His Christ.

It is not a matter then of withdrawing ourselves from signs, from the Sacraments, from the Liturgy and the Divine Word, but of discovering therein a living Presence and of being caught up in them by Its love. "The Catholic mystic is not the man who goes without all that is human in order to attain the divine . . . He is the believer for whom the theological virtues and the gifts of the Holy Spirit are so alive and purifying that he 'experiences' something of God through the signs revealed. It is not the man who turns aside from the humanity of Jesus, from the community of the Mystical Body, from the rite of the Sacraments, from the hearing of the Word of God, from contact with his brethren. It is, on the contrary, in these human realities . . . that God manifests Himself to him, dwells in him, and gives Himself to be known experimentally . . ." [2] "Contemplation is lived here, in a Church community; it is truly catholic. Such a mystic finds in the Mystery of the Church his life's environment and his guarantee." [3]

In this way we can simply affirm that the Christian mystique is a Church mystique. That is to say that for us, the search for God and the experiencing of God insofar as it is communicated to us in this life, take on life in and through the Church. It is not only the faith of the Church that sustains our progress toward God, but the actions of the Church, her Liturgy, her Sacraments, that give Him to us. To find Him, to savor Him, it is not a matter of leaving her, but of entering into her. It is a matter of performing the very actions which are the life of the Church in their fulness. It is a matter of positing them in the light of a faith to be enjoyed. It is a matter

---

[2] Rev. Fr. Plé, art. cit., p. 391.
[3] *ibid.*, p. 395.

not of raising ourselves up to God but of giving ourselves to Him in order that in these actions of the Church He may reveal His presence to us and touch us with His love. God is there in His Church; it is along with her that we must look for Him, and it is in her that we must find Him. Knowledge of the Church is the discovery of God. Perfect union with the Church is perfect union with God. The actions of the Church are the purest of prayers. The highest act of contemplation is the celebration of the Sacred Mysteries. These orientations of Church mystique have so many consequences that it is difficult to encompass them all in one glance. Let us try to set off a few of them.

First of all we must emphasize this one, which is fundamental: it is that contemplation is not a particular way, but the normal flowering of the Christian life in its perfection. It is not a special vocation but a good of the Church. We have already noted how it was inscribed in the order of development of sanctifying grace and of the gifts of the Holy Ghost, and not in that of extraordinary graces. We must say that this purely gratuitous gift of God is quite usually capable of being grafted onto the administration or reception of the Sacraments, on the daily actions of the Church, and on the realities of the apostolic life, in order to cause there the discovery of and the taste for the personal presence of Divine Love. Contemplation is not so much a particular state as it is the very life of the Christian in the Church carried to perfection; the actions of the Christian in the Church become as if transparent to themselves in order to allow a glimpse of God in His Christ . . . an experiencing of God in the Church.

It must be added that, in this perspective, far from

being opposed to apostolic activity, an authentic contemplation could quite easily be grafted onto it and lead it to its perfection. The life of the Church in us is not only the reception of grace and the welcoming of the Word, but also the transmission of the Gospel and the communication of the blessings of God. The apostle receives them to give them, "as stewards of the mysteries of God." [4]

Participation in the Divine Life not only leads us to welcome the divine blessings, but to communicate them. Supernatural relationships, the actions of the Church's life, reproduce not only the likeness of the Son Who receives the life of God, but that of the Father Who gives it. In truth, they restore to the world, at the level of relations among men, a certain participation in this communicating of life in Love which is the intimacy of the Father and the Son. The apostolic mission is grafted onto the mission of the Son and onto the Trinitary Unity. That is why the apostle who lives by this generosity of the Divine Love, and to whom God one day gives to know of this by means of a certain experience, tastes the very life of God and enters into participation in the life of the Trinity.

Thus, contemplation in the Church is not a privilege reserved to those who live in the cloister; it is not even, in the apostolic life, the privilege of hours of recollection and of rest. It is the life itself of the Church, in her prayer as well as in her action, when, having become transparent to herself, she discovers and savors for an instant, the presence of the Spirit which animates her.

Such is the intuition of the Fathers who, with St.

---

[4] 1 *Cor.* 4:1.

Gregory the Great, used to see in the Episcopate a demand for contemplation. They were right. The perfection of the Church-life which is crowned in the Bishop,
the summit of the sacramental order which is fulfilled in
the fulness of his priesthood, call forth, and so to speak
normally effect, the fulness of knowledge of the mystery
which is contemplation.

Is that not the experience of the saints? Were not the
greatest among those who gave themselves to the apostolic and missionary life, also great contemplatives? A
Saint Paul, a Saint Francis Xavier, a Saint Vincent de
Paul, a Saint Dominic, so many more! Do we not see
that far from being a sort of distraction alongside their
apostolic activity, their contemplation is its soul and
crown, that is, it supports and at times penetrates it.

Nevertheless, a difficulty comes to mind. If the richness of life in the Church is such that the graces of contemplation can be engrafted on the simplest acts of the
sacramental life, if the dignity of apostolic action is such
that it bears within itself the possibilities of authentic
contemplation, what then shall be the place of the contemplative orders in the Church, what will be the need
for recollection in the life of the apostle? Since we are
all called in the Church to this Promised Land, why set
up specialists of the contemplative life, why make it a
particular state? If all our activity can be illumined with
the wonderful experiences of Infused Wisdom, and ac-
companied by the very graces of the contemplative life,
why reserve a special time for prayer? If the whole
Church is contemplative, no more need for contemplatives! If all apostolic activity is holy and sanctifying, no
more need for recollection! These two deviations go together and threaten to accompany a poorly understood

evaluation of apostolic action. To avoid them, it would be vain not to show all the riches of contemplation in the apostolic life. But it would be imprudent not to put them in their exact places. In order to assure the necessity of prayer, it is not necessary to diminish the supernatural riches and the contemplative possibilities of action. In order to maintain the good foundation of the contemplative state in the Church, it is not of any use to question the capabilities of supernatural equilibrium in a life so completely apostolic. Quite to the contrary.

In truth, all are called to be at once contemplatives and apostles. All are called to receive the divine life and to give it. The entire life of every man must be at once recollection and radiance, receiving and giving; all to God and all to all men, because all are called to participate in the life of God in His Son Jesus, Who receives all things in order to give all things, Who belongs entirely to the Father and entirely to men, in the unity of the Spirit.

But this life is too rich to be totally expressed in everyone. It is totally expressed in Christ and is spread abroad in His Mysteries. His Mystery, the Mystery of Christ, the Paschal Mystery, the Redemptive Incarnation . . . state for us the condition, the meaning, and as it were the temporal rhythm of this life of God on earth. It is insertion and detachment, it is action and passion, it is death and life. It is assumption of humanity in order to make it pass along with Him to the Father. The Church continues the Mystery of Christ. Each of her members manifests in his way the inexhaustible riches which are hidden in Him.

It is necessary for us to know that the possession of God demands the total gift of man. He only gives Himself to those who have given everything for Him. Total detachment remains the condition for access to the goods of God. The desert is always the way which leads to the Promised Land. Poverty of heart is the only disposition required for entrance into the Kingdom of Heaven. The painful passage of the Passion is the only road which leads to the glorious Resurrection. Death is the condition of life. The stripping of the carnal man, death to the mortal world, renunciation of the desires of the flesh, is the narrow way that leads to the liberty of life according to the Spirit.

It is of this that the contemplatives are incessantly reminding us . . . not by words but by actions, not by what they say but by what they are. They have left everything. They have left the world. They are dead and they live. They are dead, their separation from every temporal function shows that; the enclosure signifies it. And they live—their joy makes us certain of it. It is necessary to die in order to live. That is certain. Their life gives us the proof of that. Dying is necessary because God is transcendent. It leads to life because He is a living God. This double assurance must be continually renewed for us. That is why the contemplative state is necessary and is part of the structure of the Church. May those be thanked who remind us at the price of their lives that man is not made solely for carrying out some function, but for the possession of the living God.

This certitude passes into every Christian life. The monk is the only one who has pushed to the limit the exigencies of his Baptism. Every baptized person can lay claim to the riches of life with God if he or she will agree to pass through death with Christ, in the way that the monk gives him the example.

Life in the world is not a refusal of the necessary detachments. It too bears its message. It transmits the good news, it announces the Gospel. It continues the Incarnation of Christ. It shows that the divine life is called, in Christ, to take possession of all human activities, to give them a new meaning and a new scope, to make them sing in praise of the Father. The retreat of the cloister is needed to show forth in the Church this death to the world which is the condition of life, to recall that the Church is adoration and praise. But Christian life in the world is necessary to show that this new life takes possession of every human reality and apostolic commitment, to bring this call to praise to every creature and to make the universe vibrate to the glory of the Creator. Thus, these two vocations are fulfilled in the Church in order to manifest in her the inexhaustible riches of the Incarnation—the mystery of a humanity entirely consecrated to God and the mystery of divine life penetrating all of humanity in Christ Jesus.

It is not enough to say that they are fulfilled; they join forces and compenetrate one another. Far from being exclusive for each person, they are ultimately complementary, because every Christian, the more he becomes himself, the more he enters into all the mystery of Christ in His Church. For the purest contemplative is also an apostle . . . and not only dreams of bearing the Gospel even to the ends of the world, but in truth does so. It is not an accident that the universal patroness of the missions is now a Saint of the great contemplative family of Carmel. But we must also say that the missionary bears in himself a secret call to the contemplative life. He is made for adoration.

The thing that differs is not the goal. All meet again

in Christ in this life of the Son which is at the same time total gift to the Father and total generosity in the service of all. In this center all are called to live of the very life of the wholly adoring and wholly apostolic Church. What is different is the state of life. For each manifests one of the aspects of the life of the Church. What is different is the way. For each ascends by a different road toward the greatly-desired goal where union with God becomes the diffusion of Charity.

For some, the total giving to God presents itself first of all as a renunciation of all the involvements of the world and a detachment from the very bonds of an apostolic charge . . . in order to manifest the absolute transcendence of Him Whom we desire. Prayer itself, which brings one close to God, makes one enter into His love for men. And it is God Who purifies the soul not only in prayer but in works. The soul that has given itself entirely to Him He turns toward others. As Fr. Marie-Eugene of the Child Jesus pointed out strongly in his study on the contemplative life,[5] the first stage of this life may well be called: "I want to see God." The second will have as its title: "I am a daughter of the Church." We know that such was the last word of the great Saint Teresa whom God led to the summits of contemplation in order to turn her to the urgent tasks of the life of the Church. The mystic who was the most detached from everything in order to belong to God alone, enters through Him into the heart of all things. She no longer acts on the periphery but through the very heart. She has found the secret of a universal apostolate: "In the heart of the Church, my mother, I want to be the love."

---

[5] Rev. Fr. Marie-Eugene de l'Enfant-Jésus, *I Want To See God* and *I am a Daughter of the Church*, Fides Publishers.

It is in this very heart that the apostle joins the contemplative. He begins, if we may so express it, from a different slope, but it is the same mountain and the same summit. Apostolic engagement also tends to total giving. He sees it first in the service of others. He renounces all the ambitions of the world, rest and personal tranquillity, to engage himself in the service of the Church. A difficult condition. The engagements of action can become temptations and solicit connivances with the world, provoke doubts regarding the mission of the Church, involve discouragements regarding his action. But we hope we have shown here that these very trials of the apostolic life have a positive meaning. They are a call to a purer search for the plan of God, a greater confidence in His grace, a more intimate discovering of the presence of Christ in His Church. They are a purification. The whole apostolic life then leads, in the rhythm of its successes and of its difficulties, to a new knowledge of Christ in His Church. It discovers progressively the face of Christ, the action of God, in the mysteries of the Church, in the acts of Liturgy, in the very actions of the apostolate. It leads to contemplation.

That is the reason that, while the contemplative life ultimately blossoms into apostolic and missionary influence, the apostolic life is fulfilled in contemplation. In order to arrive at the perfection of unity in Christ, it is necessary for the contemplative as well as for the apostle, not to leave his state to discover another, but to go to the end of his road and to live in the fulness of the grace which is apportioned out to him according to his situation in the Church. For it is life in the Church that transforms contemplatives into apostles and leads apostles to contemplation.

2. *Contemplation and position in the Church.*

Everyone admits that our apostolic activities must be measured by our position in the Church. This active part in the edification of the Mystical Body is given to us by God, and represents an aspect characteristic of our vocation. It is an appeal by God to generosity and a gift of God Who gives us the necessary graces to fulfill our mission. We have received the gift of the Holy Spirit according to the measure of Christ, each in our place, for the building up of the Body of Christ which is the Church. In this way our apostolic activity is measured by God, not with respect to our personal advancement but with respect to the good of the whole, and with respect to our position in the Church.

Why not see that it is the same way with contemplative graces? Would the Spirit Who dispenses the apostolic functions for the good of the whole, give the graces of prayer without taking the Church into account? Certainly not. The Spirit rests on the Church. If He communicates to some a little of that ineffable knowledge by which He searches the depths of God, it is in the Church and for her. As has been aptly said: "There is no experiencing of the Spirit enclosed within the limits of individuality. However personal and profound it may be, it will always remain of the Church." [6] The same Spirit Who distributes the charisms of action with respect to the structure of the Mystical Body, infuses the graces of contemplation with regard to its inmost life. There too it is correct to say with St. Paul: "In the Lord you too

---

[6] J. Mouroux, *"L'expérience chrétienne,* p. 129.

are being built together into a dwelling place for God in the Spirit." [7]

Thus our action is not an undifferentiated action, any kind of action on the part of anyone at all, but specific action, qualified by our Church position: action of pastor, of militant, of one responsible for doctrine or beneficence. Also too, our prayer, even contemplative, is qualified in the Church. It is a function of our Church position. It is not the prayer of a separated soul. It is the prayer, the offering, the adoration of a priest, a Bishop, a pastor, a militant, the head of a family. It is the transparency of a position in the Church in the light of faith and in the brilliance of gifts. It is therefore not necessary, in order to pray, to perform prayer, to contemplate, to escape from the real situation, to abstract oneself from concrete difficulties, finally, to leave behind one's apostolic responsibilities and functions. That is an indefensible undertaking, as impossible as leaping over one's shadow. We enter before God just as we are in His Church; according to our functions, as men of the Church. But the light of faith enables us to discern in this very function a mystery of God and grace enables us to consent to it. That is why the life of prayer, far from being an escape, will be consent.

In our Church situation the light of the Spirit will enable us to better discern what is of man and what is of God. It will make us discover any part of self-love, of human attachments, of carnal ambitions, that might slip into our very action. The Spirit of God will invite us to a constantly-renewed renunciation of our personal aims, in order to enter into God's plan. It will reveal to us, ulti-

---

[7] *Eph.* 2:22.

mately, this plan of God acting in the world and in our lives. It will make us taste the Infinite Love of the Father giving Itself to the world through His Christ and through the Church in which we live, in that very place where His goodness has positioned us in order to accomplish His plans of grace. And so more and more this supernatural consent to what we are and to what we do in the Church will be joined by consent to the plan of God and to the action of Christ in the world. It is by our position in the Church that we enter into the unsearchable riches of the Mercy of God manifested in Jesus His Son. In accepting this place we enter into the plan of God. And ultimately, in consenting fully to ourselves, according to God's plan, we taste the treasures of His infinite goodness for men. Our consent to ourselves according to God's plan is perfected in consent to the Church.

In this way true recollection is not a sort of abstraction from our real situation and from our apostolic functions in the Church. It is much more a deeper penetration, a more luminous view, a more loving acceptance of our Church position. That is to say it presupposes not a detachment from the body and from all social ties with the Mystical Body; but, what is totally different, detachment from the fleshly and from all the bonds of sin which attach us to worldly desires and ambitions. Yes, contemplative reflection may be considered as an anticipation of death; but not of natural death which is the disintegration of man by the separation of soul and body, but rather of that mystical death, inaugurated by Baptism, pursued throughout the Liturgy of Sacrifice, which is separation, body and soul, from this sinful world in order to enter with the Risen Christ into the Kingdom of Life.

Thus we easily understand the vital relation of prayer to the apostolic life. There is no opposition, no separation, between the two, but on the contrary, a marvelous continuity. Prayer is not a movement of the soul to God that detaches us from the earth, and the apostolate, not a movement toward men which attaches us to the world. Understood in this way, these two movements would be mutually exclusive and the apostolate would be stained with a congenital deviation.

In truth, prayer is necessary for us in order to renew each day the inmost detachment from all connivance with the sinful world, in order to illumine with the light from on high our Church position, in such wise as to see it anew not in the network of projects and ambitions of men but in the admirable deployment of God's design, to affirm the transcendence of adoration over every function and of grace over all action. The fruit of prayer will be this supernatural light on our being and on our function in the Church which will permit us to consent fully to it by seeing, and if the Spirit wills it, by tasting with joy, the marvels which love performs. From that moment, the very movement of prayer, the grace of contemplation, can pass over into apostolic action. At the price of this radical detachment that it renews and deepens, it is possible that, in the very activity in which he gives himself to others, the apostle may mysteriously experience the infinite goodness of God which passes through his heart and through his hands to spread itself in the world.

Did not Christ Himself, model of prayer and of apostolate, live incessantly in the light of vision; as well dur-

ing those nights which He would pass on the mountain
face to face with the Father, as during those days in
which He saw the Father spreading through Him the
treasures of His light and of His goodness on the miseries
and the darkness of the sinful world. Such a prayer
tends to make us see not only our personal situation, but
the whole Church, in the light of God. That is why in
this way too, we can speak here of a Church mystique.

It is not only our function, once for all defined in the
Church, in a general and as yet too abstract manner,
which is to be thus illumined. It is all our acts which are
the acts of the Church in us. To administer the Sacraments or to receive them, to perform the functions of
the Liturgy or to participate in them as a believer, to
give the instruction of the Church or to hear it, to enter
into the movements of Catholic or missionary action, all
that is indissolubly our life and the life of the Church.
That is why the contemplative grace which enables us
to discern and to taste the Presence of God and His
active love in each of our acts, enables us to recognize
Him in the very actions of His Church. Ultimately, it is
to this that it tends. It is not so much our life that it
illumines as it is the life of the Church. It is the design
of God. If this design is accomplished with an admirable
mercy even in the details of each of our functions and of
our actions, in truth it rests on the Church herself. Thus
we discover that God acts in us by reason of our adherence to His Church. We discover that the light of God
illumines our lives and transforms our action, insofar as
they belong to the Church, in such wise that if we were
to separate ourselves from the Church, our whole life,
our entire action, all our acts, would fall back into a vain
pursuing of the mirages of the world's history, into the

incoherence of its evolutions and revolutions, into the obscurity of the outer darkness. We would lose ourselves. We would no longer know what we are, nor what we are doing.

But in the measure in which we are in the Church, each of our actions finds in her an admirable meaning and a universal scope, for in each of them the mystery of the Church is accomplished and the blossoming out of catholic Charity. In each of them I contemplate and adore all the bonds of humanity with God in Christ. For each time a man kneels, it is humanity that prays in him and adores. Each time a sinner turns his face toward Him Who forgives, it is the entire Church which turns toward her Savior, Jesus. Each time a mouth is opened for Holy Communion, it is the Church herself who receives the greatly-desired Spouse Who comes each day to her. Each time, finally, that a man goes to see a poor person or a sick person in order to grant him the alms of bread or that of truth with the gift of his love and of himself, it is once again Christ Who is bending over humanity and is lifting it up in His Church.

In this way the light of God reveals in the humblest of our acts, the mystery of the Church that is being accomplished. And it is not enough to say that it is given to us to see it. We are asked to consent to it and to taste of it. For the fruit of our prayer is not simply to comprehend our life and our action such as God is guiding them, but to enter more fully into the life of the Church and to follow the impulses of the Spirit in her. It is not only to consent to ourselves in the way that God makes us, but to consent to the Church in the way God is leading her. It is to this that the Spirit leads us: to this total consent to the plan of God for the world and to what

He is presently doing in the whole Church. This puts us in our place in humility and in joy.

But this consent is not merely an adherence in words and a formula that we pronounce with our mouths. It is a giving of our whole life and an enrollment that we may perhaps have to sign with our blood. For the Word of God is efficacious, and His plan for the Church is constantly in action. We have seen that God works unceasingly on His Church in order to develop her and to make her perfect and catholic, but also to detach her and make her holy and purified. He prepares for Himself a holy Spouse, without stain, immaculate, for the Day of the Eternal Wedding. To consent to the plan of God for the Church is to enter actively into her diffusion, it is to participate in her action to spread the Gospel even to the ends of the world. But it is also to recognize and to accept the purifying action of God. It is to distinguish in the very detachments, the personal and collective detachments that are demanded of us, the law of sanctity that is operative in the Church. The mystery of the Church is the mystery of Christ, the Paschal mystery extended to the ends of the world. The Church is the place of the passage of this world to the Kingdom of Heaven. She is the Easter of this world. We must consent to pass through her or be lost. We must consent to pass with her, or attach ourselves to this world and perish with it. But rather we must admire, we must adore, we must savor, the plan of God which rests on her, the action of God which draws her, the love of God which constrains her. We must rejoice without end over the fact that through her, with her, in her, it is God Who pursues us, draws us, receives us. Our contemplation will then be, ultimately, to welcome in joy the plan of God for His

Church. Our contemplation will be to situate ourselves in the Church in order to enter into the light which illuminates her, in order to participate in the action which spreads her, in order to pass with her into the drive which carries her beyond the involvements of time to meet the Spouse Who is coming.

3. *Contemplation and hope of the Church.*

For that is the perspective that ultimately has to be set forth. Every grace of contemplation is turned to the future. This taste for the things of God which He has enabled us to experience is a foretaste of the joys of heaven. This quasi-experimental knowledge of His love is an anticipation of the eternal meetings. This light of faith which illumines the secrets of His designs and arouses admiration for the marvels He effects, is but the dawn of the great Day in which everything will at last appear in the open. This growing certainty of His invisible Presence is but the approaching of that final instant when we will at last see Him Who always sees us.

But all that is much less the fact of a particular soul and the progress of a solitary individual than the fact of the entire Church enroute to the Kingdom which is promised her since the beginning. In her we discover through contemplation, the place and the mysterious dimensions of the celestial Jerusalem. In her we perceive the earnest of those incomparable blessings, of that catholic unity, of that meeting of humanity at last re-united, of that knowledge of the Lord spread everywhere, which will constitute the light and the joy of the City of God. In her we discover at the same time, on the horizon, the outlines of the eternal shores; we already taste the first-fruits thereof, and go forward to meet joy. Our contemplation attaches itself to the Church and is nourished by her. It sees her just as she is, turned toward the eternal goods. It is in this light of hope that we understand ourselves and what we are doing in her.

The whole People of God is on the march across the desert of this world toward the riches of the Promised Land. The entire Church is being formed by this common effort toward eternal blessings. She finds her balance in this forward motion toward the new Creation that Christ will establish in the great day of His return. She herself is before us a pledge that God gives us of that new world, a sign of His action, a testimony of His faithfulness, an expectation of the great things He is preparing. Already she is beginning, in the shadows, in secret and in sorrow, this coming of God, this assembly of all people which will burst forth in joy on the Day of the Lord. All our work in the Church must be buoyed up by this hope, illumined by this contemplation.

For those of us who have charge of souls, our whole pastoral activity signifies, calls for, introduces, this definitive establishment of the Kingdom of Heaven. When we proclaim the Word of God, already that is the heralding of the ultimate effusion of the knowledge of the Father which will invade the earth as the ocean recovers the sands of the depths. When we administer the Sacraments, we bear in each of our actions, the presentiment of these eternal blessings. All these humble acts of our ministry only obtain their complete meaning and all their value if we relish in them the marvelous foretaste of the blessings which are promised to the Church.

Here is the living Jesus Who gives Himself through our hands to the entire assembled people . . . the Manna come from heaven to sustain the march to the Promised Land. But I know that whereas the appearances are expected to disappear, the reality of this act will be accomplished in the eternal. Eternally Jesus will be given to His Church, present in the depth of hearts. Eternally He will be the nourishment of every mouth which opens to receive Him. Eternally He will accomplish in Himself the unity of the assembled flock; eternally, He will be their life, their light and their joy.

In this sinner whom I pardon I see all of humanity, humanity redeemed by the Blood of the Lamb and marked with the sign of the Cross, which arises delivered from evil for a new life. In this sick person who receives the Anointing in the name of the Lord, it is all suffering humanity over which I see God bending on the last day to console it, to raise it up, to cure it. In this little one who receives the Divine Life in the fonts of Baptism I see arising a new world which flows from the hands of God for an eternal childhood. In this young man and this young woman who love each other and are bound together for life, in this joy which overflows in them, I contemplate the Spouse, the Church, meeting at last her beloved, Christ, so as to be united with Him with the indissoluble bonds of an eternal love. All the delicacy and all the strength of their human affection touch my heart with an unspeakable joy, because it bears the sign of the very love of God for this humanity, of which, in the Church, I am a part.

Why go into more detail? All our actions in the Church, our most humble actions, bear in them these infinite repercussions. Not only do I see them in this way, I live by them. And through my whole being, and by what I myself am, I bring to the world the announcement and even the accomplishment and as it were the inauguration in myself of the Kingdom of Heaven. In the Church and through her, we are bound together in the expectation and the preparation of this joy of Heaven which already comes to us and progressively takes possession of us.

And that is true not only of the ministry of the priest to which his priesthood gives a sacred sense and a supernatural scope. It is true of every act placed in the Church. It is true of the mother who nurses her little one and of this man who works to nourish his brother or to cure him, or to clothe or shelter him. For if they knew what they were doing, in truth they would know that it is with Christ Himself that they are dealing and that in them Heaven itself is already beginning. "The act of the man who buys a piece of bread at the baker's would become, if both of them knew what they are doing, as grave, as solemn, as sacred as that of two priests who, after Communion, embrace by placing their two hands on each other's shoulders." [8]

What is missing to us is not Christ, it is the sense of His presence which will be revealed to us on the last day when it will be said to us: "Whatsoever you have done to the least of my brethren you have done it to me," and we will have to admit that it was true. In this way not only all ministry in the Church, but ultimately all labor and all true love in the world, bears in itself the expectation and the preparation of the eternal encounters. "How they love one another without knowing it, and how wonderful it would be if they did know it! What they do without knowing I would like them to do know-

---

[8] P. Claudel, *Positions et propositions*, II, p. 47, Ed. Gallimard.

ingly." [9] That is why, unceasingly, our contemplation is rooted in the life of the Church and is nourished by her actions.

The Church alone reveals to the world what she is doing. She gives that its meaning and discovers it its goal. In her we contemplate the new world which is being prepared and toward which all things conspire. In her we discover this new humanity at last re-united, the bonds of which all human encounters are preparing in secret. In her we work without cease for the establishment of that justice and Charity the unquenchable thirst which pursues us even to the Day of the Last Judgment. In her we see growing the city whose foundations are built on this earth but whose crowning pieces will come down from heaven. In her we receive a new being and a new birth. We receive the light to see the world as it must be, and we receive the life to become what we will be eternally. A new world is developing, for which she furnishes the material and which the Spirit fructifies in her. For it is in her that we have received forever a new life and our name for eternity. She is our mother, we are her sons and death itself can no longer separate us.

---

[9] P. Claudel, *Conversation dand le Loir-et-Cher*, p. 102.

FINIS